POSITIONED FOR PROMOTION

POSITIONED FOR PROMOTION

HOW TO INCREASE YOUR INFLUENCE AND CAPACITY TO LEAD

by

Mac Hammond

Harrison House
Tulsa, Oklahoma

Positioned for Promotion—
How To Increase Your Influence and Capacity To Lead
ISBN 1-57794-329-5
Copyright © 2000 by Mac Hammond
P.O. Box 29469
Minneapolis, MN 55429

Published by Harrison House, Inc.
P. O. Box 35035
Tulsa, Oklahoma 74135

CONTENTS

Section 3 *The Successful Communicator*

Section 4 *The Mandate To Motivate*

Epilogue

INTRODUCTION

For promotion cometh neither from the east, nor from the west, nor from the south.

But God is the judge: he putteth down one, and setteth up another.

Psalm 75:6

Is it okay to want a promotion? Does God mind if you want to move up the ladder and enjoy some of the perks that come with increased responsibility?

Many people, particularly Christians, can't answer either of these questions with confidence. They are inwardly conflicted. On one hand, they have the desire to achieve and to lead. On the other hand, they've been told that success in this life is not a valid option for them.

The truth is (and this is a truth I want to hammer home in this book), your desires to achieve and win are God-given. He wants His people to succeed. In other words, it's okay to want a promotion.

God wants to position you for promotion.

One problem is that in the twenty-first-century economy, the work world is radically changing. For the average person working in the secular world, the path of promotion has never been more unclear. The fact is, there is a wide gap between what most people assume will get them promoted and what managers are actually thinking.

For example, Sandy J. Wayne, a management professor at the University of Illinois at Chicago, recently asked 570 employees and 289 managers at a large U.S. company to rank the most important factors influencing promotions.

For the employees, having a degree from a top school came first. Their bosses, on the other hand, gave leadership skills first place. Employees also gave a high rank to having a mentor. Yet executives hardly mentioned this at all—they looked for a strong work ethic instead.[1]

So how do you get past the discrepancies and catch up with the new thinking on getting promotions? By basing your life and actions on eternal principles.

God's principles of promotion will work in any economy, in any era and for any person bold enough to apply them. That's what this book is all about.

As you read, my prayer is that you'll gain the biblical insights and eternal wisdom principles that will increase your influence, expand your capacity to lead and propel you to your highest destiny in God.

May you be positioned for promotion.

SECTION 1

Godly Leadership

1

CALLED TO LEADERSHIP

Let me begin with a statement that may surprise you.

If you are a born-again believer, you are called to be a leader. I can say that with confidence because I know your eternal destiny as a Christian is to rule and reign with Jesus. The truth is, our life on this earth is simply a preparatory stage for how we will spend eternity.

I hate to be the one to burst your bubble if you have seen yourself in heaven, lying in your hammock sipping a glass of iced tea. The Lord has plans for you. According to the Word of God, you are going to be ruling, reigning and governing with Him, not just for a thousand years during the Millennium, but for eternity. And right now you are being prepared for the leadership position you will hold in the Kingdom of God.

The little-known fact is that we must learn leadership principles for our eternal destiny and to achieve God's best in this life.

At this point you may be saying, "But, Mac, I don't have the traditional leader's personality." That doesn't matter. You can influence others with any personality style, and as we're about to learn, influence is synonymous with leadership.

AN OVERLOOKED PRINCIPLE

One of the basic principles of Christianity, often overlooked in our busyness, is that we shouldn't be satisfied with the status quo in any area of our lives. We are never to be satisfied with the state of our health. (You can always be fitter.) We are never to be satisfied with the state of our finances. (We must always reach for more in order to spread the Gospel.)

The saying "I'm just satisfied with my lot in life" is a bunch of baloney. You shouldn't be. You should always be reaching higher.

Paul said it this way:

Brethren, I count not myself to have apprehended: but this one thing I do, forgetting those things which are behind, and reaching forth unto those things which are before, I press toward the mark for the prize of the high calling of God in Christ Jesus.

Philippians 3:13,14

We should be pressing. We should never be satisfied. We should press toward those values we see in the life of Jesus. He was a man of love, and He walked in love; therefore, we must press toward improving our love walk.

When we see His compassion, we must desire to be compassionate after the same fashion. We see His strength, so we must press toward being strong—or patient, or full of faith and power—as Jesus was. But, we should not press toward only one or two of His characteristics. We should press toward all of them.

Among Jesus' attributes, His leadership abilities have never been emphasized enough. Yet in the space of three short years, His ministry changed the face of this earth like nothing else ever has.

We must study His example of leadership, begin to emulate it and press toward developing those same leadership characteristics in our lives. In so doing, we press toward the mark in an area the body of Christ has long neglected.

Why have we neglected this area for centuries? I believe the major cause is rooted in an ancient and widespread "religious" deception.

THE OLD WORM COMPLEX

One of the greatest deceptions Satan ever perpetrated on the body of Christ is the "old worm complex." This is the mindset which says, *I'm just an old sinner saved by grace.* It is a lie which keeps more people from stepping out into the leadership role God has prepared for them. It causes them to sit back and just wait for the Lord to return and to accept whatever fate the Devil brings them.

> *To be a conqueror, you must be a leader. If you aren't, you will be a follower, never changing anything.*

This is one of the reasons for which we have not had a greater impact on this world; it is why Christianity has not already changed the face of this globe to an extent sufficient to bring the Lord back. This self-image problem has developed as a result of the Devil's lie.

The result is that God's army is filled with a bunch of career privates. Did you get that? What the Devil has done with this particular deception in the is to fill God's army with a bunch of career privates. In other words, they fill their place in God's army but never advance.

To be a conqueror, you must be a leader. If you aren't, you will be a follower, never changing anything.

ALL CHIEFS AND NO INDIANS

How can everyone be a leader? Wouldn't we then be a church of all chiefs and no Indians? To answer that you must understand two things about leadership. First, there are many different levels and types of leadership. Second, everybody cannot lead in the same place at the same time. However, everybody is called to lead at different levels and in different places over a period of time.

Consider an army for a moment. At any point they have hundreds of privates, all in rank divisions. There are privates, third, second and first class; corporals; about four or five levels of sergeants on up to the commissioned ranks. Then you have second and first lieutenants, captains, majors, lieutenant colonels, colonels and four or five different types of generals. The many, many rank divisions represent levels of leadership.

Also, because of retirement (and other forms of attrition), casualties and discharge, there are always new recruits coming in. Officer Candidate School and the U.S. Military Academy at West Point are always filled with replacements for the officers who leave, just as new enlistees replace the non-commissioned officers.

It is the same in God's army—the body of Christ.

DIFFERENT LEVELS, DIFFERENT TYPES

In the body of Christ, the different levels of authority are continually changing. People are graduating to new levels, retiring from active duty or dying and going home to be with the Lord. Things happen which open new slots that God must move someone into if the leadership of the ranks is to continue smoothly. He is looking for you. He does not want you to be a career private.

One of our problems is that nobody really understands the different types of leadership positions there are. We hear somebody talk about leadership and we instantly think of someone directing a large group of people, such as a business or a corporation or perhaps a ministry. But leadership begins at a much more basic and generally unacknowledged level. God requires you to be faithful in the fundamentals in order for you to be promoted. And the most fundamental level of leadership begins at your own doorstep. I'm talking about the family.

FAMILY LEADERSHIP

Family is probably one of the most critical areas of influence in which any of us will exercise our leadership responsibilities—whether it is as the husband God has designated as the head of the home or the wife God has called to manage the home and raise the children. The family unit is an important place of leadership in the body of Christ.

In the context of a family, the Lord gives us a hint about promotion in His kingdom and in His army. He says that if a man does not rule his house well, he has no business seeking to become a bishop in the church or looking for a position somewhere else. (1 Tim. 3:1-5.)

In other words, you must start out being faithful at home in order to lead effectively at the level of responsibility God has given you—and then He will promote you.

In every relationship you have, there is an opportunity for you to be a leader. Every back-fence conversation in which you give direction to someone's life is an example of leadership and of your participation in it. As you are faithful to respond in these little opportunities, God will present you with more and more opportunities for leadership.

2

CHARACTERISTICS
OF GODLY LEADERSHIP

Not every effective leader is a godly leader. Hitler was highly effective at motivating others, yet he was evil and unimaginably destructive.

The first reason for knowing the characteristics of godly leadership is so you do not mistakenly follow ungodly leaders. An example of this is the Jonestown affair, in which over 900 followers committed mass suicide under cult leader Jim Jones' direction.

It was tragic that a man, so deceived, led those people off to their deaths. But even more tragic was that all those people followed him unquestioningly.

In order to grow as a leader, you must be able to think and evaluate leadership on your own. You must know what kind of leadership you are committing to. Learning the characteristics of godly leadership will prevent you from being led off like those people in the Jim Jones cult.

The second reason for knowing the characteristics of godly leadership is so that you can evaluate your own leadership development. You are called to be a leader, so you must have some measure for evaluating your development as a leader.

Well, what are the characteristics of godly leaders?

FINAL AUTHORITY

The first and most basic characteristic of scriptural leadership is that the Word of God must be the final authority in your decision-making process. Not external circumstances, not what you see with your natural eyes, not the prevailing policies and practices of the moment, but the Word of God must be the final authority.

It is the same as when you are saved. You are not going to be saved by listening to someone's opinion. You are going to be saved by hearing, believing and confessing the Word of God.

The same is true in leading people or in making the decisions a leader is required to make. The Word of God has to be the final authority. It has to be the basis of our leadership. Anything else will lead to disaster.

Let us look at the familiar story of the men sent to spy out Canaan before Moses took the children of Israel into the Promised Land. I want you to see some things in this story which relate to leadership.

> **And the Lord spake unto Moses, saying, Send thou men, that they may search the land of Canaan, which I give unto the children of Israel: of every tribe of their fathers shall ye send a man, every one a ruler among them.**
>
> **Numbers 13:1,2**

LEADERSHIP LEADS THE WAY

God told Moses to send leadership—men who were rulers among them—and Moses, by the commandment of the Lord, sent them to the wilderness of Paran. The men who were sent to spy out the land were the leaders of the children of Israel.

When the spies returned, Caleb and Joshua were so excited about what they had seen, they stood up and said, "Hey, God said we could take this land. Let's go do it." Numbers 13:30 tells us, **And Caleb stilled the people before Moses, and said, Let us go up at once and possess it; for we are well able to overcome it.**

How do you think he knew that? Because God had told him they would. (Num. 13:2.) God had already given them the land.

But the men that went up with him said, We be not able to go up against the people; for they are stronger than we. And they brought up an evil report of the land which they had searched unto the children of Israel, saying, The land, through which we have gone to search it, is a land that eateth up the inhabitants thereof; and all the people that we saw in it are men of a great stature. And there we saw the giants, the sons of Anak, which come of they giants; and we were in our own sight as grasshoppers, and so we were in their sight.

Numbers 13:31-33

YOUR BASIS FOR SETTING LIMITS

Now we know that this land *was* in fact populated with giants, but God had said He would give them the land *in spite of* the giants. So the leadership of the children of Israel did not decide on the basis of God's Word; instead they decided on the basis of what they saw. The spies saw giants. And the result of their refusal to obey God's Word was to wander in the wilderness for forty years.

No group or organization—not even God's chosen people—can grow beyond its leadership.

For example, as a general rule, God wants the churches He initiates to explode, to take the Word to all of the world. He does not want hundreds of little "bless me" clubs scattered all over the city or the country. He wants the churches He initiates to grow by winning souls to the Lord and proclaiming the Kingdom of God.

When you see a church or a ministry that is stagnant, you can know it has gone as far as its leadership has been willing to take it.

The key to growth in any organization or family is simple. Leaders must base their decisions on what God says, not on what man says.

A BASIS FOR BUILDING

When we were planning for a new building at the church I pastor, the vice president of the leasing division of a banking institution came from Chicago to meet with the developer of the complex in which we wanted to build. He told that developer (who happened to owe $4 million in notes which were coming up for renewal in two weeks), "If you let that church into this industrial complex, we're not going to renew those $4 million worth of notes. A church has no business being in an industrial complex. It's the most ridiculous thing I have ever heard."

Well, I met with the man and gave him a beautiful ten-minute sermon, explaining why the spot we had picked was perfect for our church. And do you know what he did? He mocked God. He even cursed and said as far as he was concerned, he would never change his mind.

So the man left, and we proceeded with our plans. We kept the architect working on the plans, and we put our "pray-ers" on a twenty-four-hour watch.

About a week and a half later, for no plausible reason, the man from Bank of America called the developer and said, "Well, it's all right. Let the church in."

This man had been so adamant against our having a church in that complex—there wasn't any way he was going to change his mind! But it only took about a week and a half for God to change it. A big giant fell!

A BASIS FOR FLYING

All I am saying is that you should do what God tells you, not what the world tells you, not what circumstances would seem to dictate.

When the ruler Jairus received the report that his daughter was dead, he didn't listen to that report; he listened to Jesus, who said, **Believe only** (Luke 8:50).

Faith is acting on your belief. The Lord will take care of the rest. When church or business leaders—or you as the leader of your family—act on what God says, not what the world says, the blessings come.

A trip we took to Washington is another good example of the blessings of following God's Word.

The DC9 we wanted to charter was only half full, yet we were supposed to pay $27,000 for it. At that point we had the opportunity to gracefully cancel our plans and tell everybody, "We'll see you there. Just make your own flight plans and go on. This didn't work out."

> *When church or business leaders—or you as the leader of your family—act on what God says, not what the world says, the blessings come.*

But God had spoken to us. He'd said, "Charter that jet and fill it up with believers."

So we took a deep breath and went ahead and paid the costs out of the church reserves. Sure enough, every seat on that plane filled up, and we did not lose a cent. We were even able to send a lot of people free of charge.

For a leader to be blessed by God, His Word must be the final authority.

3

SEPARATED UNTO LEADERSHIP

Everyone in the body of Christ is called to some level of leadership; however, just because we are called to be leaders does not mean we should seek leadership positions.

God does the calling as well as the separating. He places the desire in your heart and the call on your life. You might have the desire to serve Him for years before the call is completely fulfilled, but in His timetable, He will see to it that doors open for you.

Are you wondering how to know when you should step into a leadership position? Here is the key to His separation to leadership: He will bring across your path an opportunity to accept responsibility, to accomplish a task which will invariably involve others' working in a support role. It might be a small task at first, or it may be bigger than you think you are ready to tackle.

In any event, you will have the opportunity to accept it and move into a leadership role or to reject it and stay a career private. The choice will be yours. God provides an opportunity to step into a position of responsibility. But, ultimately, the choice is yours.

AUTHORITY AND RESPONSIBILITY

There are a lot of folks who are authority seekers. They want to be able to say, "You do this," or "You do that," or "Brother, I have a word for you." But you cannot rightfully assume authority without first being given responsibility.

Let me give you an example. As a parent, you have been given the responsibility for your children. So you have the authority to administer discipline to them. Do you have the authority to run over and apply the rod to your neighbor's children? Of course not! (Although you might wish you did!)

But, the fact of the matter is that you have no responsibility for their lives. Your neighbor has been given the responsibility for raising those children in the nurture and admonition of the Lord. (Eph. 6:4.) You cannot run over there and exercise authority over them. No responsibility means no authority.

It works the same in the Kingdom of God. Responsibility always precedes authority. Yet, we have people trying to exercise authority when God has not given them the responsibility. Really what they are doing is usurping authority that belongs to someone else. That creates problems in any group or organization or body.

The apostle John says an authority seeker **loveth to have the preeminence among men** (3 John 9). These people are prone to strife and malicious words. They are never content with what another leader does. They seek authority over people; control is the bottom line. Stay away from this kind of person. Nothing good will come of an association with them.

THE KEY TO LEADERSHIP

The key to exercising appropriate leadership authority is being faithful in the areas in which God has given you responsibility. For most of us that begins in the family unit. Just be patient and allow Him to promote you from there.

Luke 16:12 sets forth a principle regarding responsibility and promotion in the Kingdom of God. **And if ye have not been faithful in that which is another man's, who shall give you that which is your own?**

Maybe you are an employee in another man's business. The profitability of that business is his responsibility. If you are faithful to function to the point that you contribute to that profitability, you are proving your faithfulness to him and his area of responsibility. Eventually you are going to be given that which is your own: your own department, your own division, maybe even your own business. But you must first be faithful to someone else's responsibility; then God will promote you.

This is a principle seen throughout the Word of God. You must first serve in order to qualify for leadership.

We know Jesus was the greatest leader the world has ever known. Yet, didn't He also wash His disciples' feet? Didn't He also say He was a servant? This world-changer told His followers He came to serve, not to be served, and then He washed their feet.

PAUL'S QUALIFICATIONS

Let's move forward into the Church age and see how Paul qualified his leaders. In Philippians 2, Paul prepared the church at Philippi for a visit from Timothy. As an emissary from Paul, Timothy had a lot of responsibility, as well as authority. Paul told the church of Timothy's qualifications for leadership, beginning in verse 20:

> **For I have no one like him—no one of so kindred a spirit—who will be so genuinely interested in your welfare and devoted to your interests. For the others all seek [to advance] their own interests, not those of Jesus Christ, the Messiah.**
>
> **But Timothy's tested worth you know, how as a son with his father he has toiled with me zealously [serving and helping to advance] the good news (the Gospel).**
>
>

Philippians 2:20-22 AMP

Make note of this. Being a servant and taking a genuine interest in those over whom God makes you responsible is how you qualify for authority in the Kingdom of God.

Do you have a business? Are you genuinely interested in the welfare of your employees? Or are you basically motivated to generate a profit only for yourself?

Are you in ministry? I could ask the same questions. Do you have a genuine interest in the people who are called to be a part of your work for God, or should you ask the Lord for more compassion?

What about your family? Do you have a genuine interest in your kids and in what they do? Do you have your spouse's best interests at heart? Are you willing to serve them in such a way that they will become what God wants, rather than what you want? If your church had a foot-washing service, could you wash the feet of your children? Your spouse?

According to the Word of God, these are the basic qualifications for advancement and promotion in the Kingdom of God.

LEADERSHIP, NOT DRIVERSHIP

God's leaders will never force, intimidate, coerce or push anyone into doing anything. Have you heard the saying, "You don't drive sheep; you drive cattle. You lead sheep"? Shepherds lead, and the sheep follow. That means you must be out front, setting the example, in whatever arena you are a leader. First Peter 5:3 says, **Neither as being lords over God's heritage, but being ensamples** [examples] **to the flock.** You must lead by example.

If, as a pastor, I have no desire to see people born again, or if I have the desire but will not translate that desire into action through witnessing and praying with people, how can I expect my church to be a soulwinning church? How can I expect my flock to do what I, as their shepherd, will not do?

Thank God the blood of Jesus cleanses me from my sin, and I can ask my children for forgiveness and start over with them as well.

There are occasions when I have to get on my face and repent. Say, for example, that I go home one day as "the big pastor," having just saved a falling marriage with my wonderful counseling. If then one of my kids does something wrong and I lose my temper and shout at them, how can I tell them not to lose their temper? It simply doesn't work.

Thank God the blood of Jesus cleanses me from my sin, and I can ask my children for forgiveness and start over with them as well. But what is important is that we gain the wisdom of an old proverb my grandfather used to quote, "Sometimes what you do speaks so loudly that others cannot hear what you are saying."

Remember, God separates you unto leadership; He gives you the opportunities to prove yourself faithful.

4

GENTLENESS

He shall feed his flock like a shepherd; he shall gather the lambs with his arm, and carry them in his bosom, and shall gently lead those that are with young.

Isaiah 40:11

One characteristic of godly leadership which many of us miss is gentleness. The reason I missed it for so long is that I was raised with the idea that a man has to be a tough guy. He cannot show any emotion. He cannot show any concern or compassion for people. He has to be a hard-liner. He can't mince words with people just because he cares about them. He has to make them tow the line!

So as a man and a leader, discipline was the name of my game. And if someone missed it, I felt I had to get on their case hard so they would not miss it again. As you can see, I had some real changing to do when I began to learn more about godly leadership.

Gentleness is not an unmasculine trait; it is not a sign of weakness for a man or a woman. As a matter of fact, properly understood, real gentleness springs from confidence in your strength and in the ability of Jesus which resides in you by the power of His Holy Spirit. It is confidence which comes from walking in the knowledge that you need not feel threatened that somebody might usurp your power or your authority.

On the other hand, shouting loud, abrasive directions is a sign of insecurity and perceived inferiority. Many leaders possess an unshakable firmness, but gentleness is a sign of strength that can come only from God. It is a characteristic of true godly leadership.

GOD IS A GENTLEMAN

God will never override your will, even if it means seeing you go unsaved. You are a free moral agent, and you can go to hell if you choose to. But this would grieve Him.

It tears God's heart apart when someone rejects Him. He would rather rejoice over the sinner who comes into the Kingdom. But He will not impose on your will in order to bring you into His Kingdom. Even though He gave Jesus for you, He will allow you to live a life totally opposed to the principles He has set forth in His Word. And He will ultimately allow you to go to hell if you make that choice. He respects your free will that much.

We see this same gentlemanly trait in the apostle Paul. Now, Paul carried a lot of clout with the churches where he ministered. But even so, he followed the biblical example—he would not coerce a brother into doing something he did not want to do. **As touching our brother Apollos, I greatly desired him to come unto you with the brethren: but his will was not at all to come at this time; but he will come when he shall have convenient time** (1 Cor. 16:12).

Strong leadership—godly leadership—does not override someone else's will.

CONCERNING SIN

Thus far, I have been describing situations in which sin is not involved. Paul dealt with sin in an entirely different fashion. He was not tolerant of sin or the Devil. He was not tolerant of situations where someone's disobedience could affect other people. Neither is God.

You can do anything you want as far as God is concerned as long as it does not affect others negatively. In other words, you can send yourself to hell, and God will not stop you. However, when your behavior begins to influence others to go along with you, He takes action.

For example, if you have a rebellious child, you cannot force him to quit smoking pot. You can wear out his rear end all you want; you can ground him for life; but you cannot force him to abstain if he has a mind to do it anyway. The same is true with any other form of disobedience. So what do you do?

Well, if you have other children and one child's disobedience and rebellion is affecting the others negatively, you have to take strong steps to stop the one, even though it might be against his will.

Just know that God doesn't allow other people to be affected negatively either. A friend of mine actually had to put his sixteen-year-old out of their home because of the terrible effect his behavior was having on his younger brothers and sisters.

There must be a balance. Paul did not wink at sin. Neither does God, and neither should you.

But within the parameters of managing or leading others who are your responsibility, leadership by force is not the way to do it.

IMITATING GOD'S STYLE

What is God's style? How does He draw you to Himself when you are behaving badly? He does it by sending laborers to witness to you, to change you with the Word by bringing light and understanding into your life. And that is precisely what a godly leader will do; he will use the Word of God.

In the case of my friend's son, it was a godly grandmother who changed the rebellious boy's behavior.

If you are a leader, whether it be a family or a large corporation, your leadership success will come only in obtaining the voluntary and willing support and service of those whom you lead.

This was certainly the case with another of the Bible's successful leaders—Gideon. Judges 8:22 tells us, **Then the men of Israel said unto Gideon, Rule thou over us, both thou and thy son, and thy son's son also; for thou hast delivered us from the hand of Midian.**

Gideon was a just, godly man. His actions resulted in blessing and deliverance for the entire nation of Israel. They *wanted* him to rule over them. A characteristic of godly leadership will always be that those whom you lead will voluntarily submit to your leadership.

Gideon's response to the people was, **I will not rule over you, neither shall my son rule over you: the Lord shall rule over you** (Judg. 8:23).

And therein lies the most important key to understanding godly leadership: It is not the person standing up in front who is ultimately leading you. He or she is only a vessel chosen of God for the Lord's power to flow through, so God can impart direction to your life. God is the one who is ruling over you through that person. As Gideon said, "God is in charge, not I."

This is a truth every leader must recognize and embrace. It is not by the might or the strength or the power of your hand that you rule. You "rule" by your obedience to the Lord, the One who leads through you.

QUALIFIED FOR LEADERSHIP

In 1 Timothy, Paul outlines the qualifications for godly leadership. If you have not yet been separated by God to a greater level of responsibility and authority in the body of Christ, you will want to check this list and see if you fall short in some area. Remember, God will not promote you until you are qualified. This list will give you something to work toward, change or improve so that the Lord can move you higher.

In 1 Timothy 3, we discover the qualifications for being a bishop. Qualifications for leadership in general can be extracted from these same verses of Scripture: **A bishop then must be blameless, the husband of one wife** (v. 2).

Now, this does not mean (as some have claimed) that those who have been divorced cannot be leaders, nor does it mean a woman cannot qualify for a leadership position. The Word is telling us that in a universal sense, a leader—man or woman—if married, must be married to only one person.

> *The Word is telling us that in a universal sense, a leader—man or woman—if married must be married to only one person.*

This verse has been used to keep a lot of church people from serving God. They say, "Hey! You can't be an usher. You can't be a deacon. You can't be anything in the church because you've been divorced." That is not what Paul is saying. Polygamy was commonplace in his day and time, so Paul was simply saying, "If you are going to be a leader and you are married, your marriage must be right before God."

This, however, isn't the only qualification Paul mentions here.

VIGILANCE

A bishop then must be . . . vigilant, sober, of good behaviour, given to hospitality, apt to teach; not given to wine, no striker, not greedy of filthy lucre; but patient, not a brawler, not covetous; one that ruleth well his own house, having his children in subjection with all gravity; (For if a

man know not how to rule his own house, how shall he take care of the church of God?) Not a novice, lest being lifted up with pride, he fall into the condemnation of the devil.

1 Timothy 3:2-6

There are a lot of interesting terms in this list. Let's examine each one of them.

The word *vigilant* means watchful. A leader cannot be lazy.

To be *sober* means to not be given to foolishness.

The phrase *Of good behavior* means one always acts becomingly.

Given to hospitality means one must be able to be with people for fellowship as well as for ministry.

Apt to teach simply means one is able to teach.

Not given to wine means one avoids the pitfalls of alcohol consumption.

No striker is an old English term that means one does not make hasty covenants for the purpose of gain.

Not greedy of filthy lucre means one is not unduly motivated by financial gain.

To be *patient* means to be steady in the face of adverse circumstance.

Not a brawler means not losing your temper or getting in fights.

Not covetous means not wishing you had what belongs to someone else.

One that ruleth well his own house: As I have already pointed out, you can't lead an organization if your own family is out of control.

The phrase *not a novice* means not a new believer. If a person was born again two months ago, God isn't going to make him a pastor next month. Nor will He put him in a position of authority in the body of Christ until he has had time to grow and mature in the Lord. And when he has grown up in the things of God, if he is prideful, God still will not put him in a position of authority.

Verse 7 continues, **Moreover he must have a good report of them which are without.** The term *without* refers to those outside the body of Christ—the unsaved world. Someone who has a terrible reputation with "them that are without" may get gloriously born again, but that report must change before the person is elevated to a position of authority.

It always saddens me when I see people who have just come out of a life of crime or depravity elevated to a position of importance in the local body, simply because of their marvelous testimony. God warns against that. He says their testimony must be proven and established over time, **lest he fall into reproach, and the snare of the devil** (v. 7).

Now let's examine the qualifications for being a deacon, so you can see the importance of having strong, personal development before entering a leadership role.

> **Let the deacons be the husbands of one wife, ruling their children and their own houses well. For they that have used the office of a deacon well, purchase to themselves a good degree, and great boldness in the faith which is in Christ Jesus.**
>
> **1 Timothy 3:12,13**

That "great boldness" gives you even more opportunity to influence people through your leadership.

Paul is very specific in his teaching on the qualifications for leadership. Meditating on those qualifications will help you determine whether or not you are ready for promotion to greater responsibility or show you why you might not be getting promoted as you think you should.

Above all, we need to remember that godly leadership requires gentleness.

5

HONOR:
A LEADER'S GREATEST TOOL

As we've seen in previous chapters, we lead by serving and we lead by loving. But there is another vital element that only the most effective leaders possess. It's an element that hasn't received a lot of attention in the leadership literature that fills the shelves of your local bookstore.

This element goes hand in hand with serving and loving and actually makes them come alive. It's the Bible word *honor*.

The Greek word translated *honour* in the New Testament connotes something of priceless value. This word is associated with a sense of heaviness and weightiness. It's similar to glory in one respect. And when you learn to give honor to people, you open them to your influence in remarkable ways. Honor is a powerful biblical principle.

Frankly, honor is the key to making any relationship work. And as a leader, it is perhaps one of your most important tools in opening another person's life and heart to your influence and to the direction

God would bring through you. Of course, it can't be something you use in a manipulative sense. No, this is a genuine thing I'm talking about. I'm referring to making a quality decision to honor other people. This is the element that is so frequently missing in the lives of leaders.

Of course, you can serve and love without honoring somebody. But it's not scriptural love. It's not scriptural service. Because when you serve somebody without the element of honor, essentially you're saying, "I'm serving you because the Bible says I must, but deep down I don't want to."

I'm here to let you know that it won't work. That's not scriptural service. It's not scriptural love, and it won't produce the result the Bible promises.

I have discovered this about biblical love: It is a reflection of how much you value another person. That's all. Your willingness to serve on a long-term basis is a reflection of how much you value whomever it is you're serving. So love really is an outworking of your decision to place a priceless value on the people that God brings into your life.

"But Mac," you might say, "what if a person doesn't deserve any honor. How can you give honor to somebody to whom honor really isn't due?"

I would respond by reminding you that this is precisely what God did for each one of us. He valued us so much that He paid the ultimate price. Did you deserve it? Of course you didn't. Nor did I. So to say that we can't honor somebody until they've become deserving of it is inconsistent with the example Jesus set for us.

God has already demonstrated to us that it is His purpose for us to extend honor—to place a high value on the people He brings into our lives, whether they deserve it or not. Why? Because He loves us that way too.

HONOR OPENS THE DOOR

Once you decide that you're going to honor somebody and you then begin doing the things that will honor them, you open them to your influence and leadership. You open them to receive direction they can follow with their whole hearts.

To open people to your leadership, you must honor them. It's a principle we find woven throughout Scripture.

We know that the Word instructs us to honor God. He also tells husbands to honor their wives. (1 Peter 3:7.) In the same chapter, wives are exhorted to honor their husbands. Of course, children are repeatedly commanded in Scripture to honor their parents. (A great promise comes with that command—long life and good health.) And in Romans 12:10, all believers are encouraged to prefer one another "in honour."

In none of these instances does the instruction to give honor have anything to do with whether or not the person deserves it. God didn't put a condition on it. He just said do it.

I believe that honor is frequently the missing element where our interpersonal relationships are concerned. And yet, according to the Word, it's the one thing that will unlock a person's heart so you can become effective in your leadership.

So practically speaking, how do you honor people?

KEYS TO GIVING HONOR

Some of the most important aspects of giving honor have already been mentioned—having the attitude of a servant-leader and in the decision-making process, for example. That makes the well-being of those you lead the primary consideration in decision making, rather than your own job security or your own future. When that's genuinely your view of things, you are honoring them. You're esteeming them highly. You're making a declaration of their value.

Once you become honor-conscious in your interactions with others, you'll find many opportunities to be so as you go about the routine of your day. For example, when you ignore another person's questions or opinions, you dishonor him, don't you? Or if you belittle a person's opinions or views, you've dishonored her, haven't you?

To my embarrassment, I must confess to you that I've been guilty of that on a number of occasions. More than once, someone has tendered an opinion to me, and, in the press of urgent daily business, I didn't even respond to it. I now know that to do so was really a point of dishonor to that person. My actions said, "I don't value you." Of course, that wasn't an accurate reflection of the reality in my heart.

Once I've dishonored someone, I've closed him to me a little. I've started closing his heart to my influence and leadership.

Obviously, one of the ways to honor someone is to simply be courteous enough to listen to and acknowledge another's opinion, saying something like, "Hey, I really appreciate that. That's a good idea. I'm going to pray about that. I don't know if it will fit or work, but I'm going to take this to the Lord. We're going to consider it, and I thank you for bringing me that."

That's honoring them.

On the other hand, you can dishonor someone by not giving him your full attention when he's trying to tell you something. You've probably had it happen to you, and if you're like me, you don't care for it one bit. You're in someone's presence and you're trying to tell him something, but he's looking out the window or scanning for someone else he needs to speak to. It's simply a lack of honor being displayed.

In what other ways do we dishonor people? Let's examine the thorny subject of correction for a moment.

If you lead for any length of time, you're sure to encounter situations in which you have to correct somebody. The key is to do it without dishonoring him. How can you point out something he's done wrong without demeaning or devaluing him?

Obviously, you must avoid giving the correction in anger. It's possible to be firm without being harsh. Beyond this, it is important to make sure your message isn't judgmental or harshly critical. Attack the behavior, not the person. Point out the mistake in judgment, rather than questioning the person's intelligence.

Jesus gives us wonderful examples of delivering correction in His letters to the churches of Asia Minor in Revelation 2 and 3.

> *Point out the mistake in judgment, rather than questioning the person's intelligence.*

To the church at Ephesus in chapter 2, he starts out by saying, "I know thy works and how you have labored for my name." He goes for a whole verse telling them all of the good things they've done. He honors them and then he says in essence, "Nevertheless, there is something we need to deal with." (vv. 1-4.)

If you're quick to give praise and recognition for contributions made—if you are consistent in honoring people for genuine efforts and good things done—then when it comes time to correct, you can do so without devaluing them.

Finally, one of the most common ways leaders dishonor those they are leading is through a failure to say two simple words—*thank you.*

It's easy to take for granted the contributions and efforts of those around you. If you don't express appreciation for all that's done for you, then you're greatly dishonoring the people who serve you. You're demeaning their efforts. You're devaluing their loyalty and their efforts to help you.

I don't care how high you've climbed in the organization or how many people are accountable to your authority; you never get so important that you can excuse yourself from being thankful and appreciative for the things that people do for you.

YOUR GREATEST TOOL—USE IT

To me this is one of the leaders' greatest tools for accessing the whole-hearted support, loyalty and cooperation of those who are a part of your life. If you take the time to honor them as valuable—treasures God has entrusted to your care—and if you approach them that way, I am absolutely confident it will stand you in good stead. It will make you a true servant-leader. And as we've seen, servant-leadership is the paradigm of leadership the Bible gives us. It's the only one that will always succeed.

6

PRINCIPLES OF LEADERSHIP

Let's say God has called you to a leadership role. What now? Does it just automatically happen? Do you just fall into it? Not quite. God gives you some very basic principles to follow in order to ensure your success as a leader in the Kingdom of God.

You can see these principles operating in the lives of all the great leaders in the Bible. You can see them in the lives of Moses and Joshua. You can see them in the life of Paul and in the life of Jesus Himself. These were all men whom people wanted to follow. Men who gave their followers direction and then motivated them to action.

NOT ALONE

If you are going to be an effective leader, the first thing people must see is that God is with you. In Exodus 3, God appeared to Moses in a burning bush and told him to deliver His people from bondage in Egypt.

Moses immediately began to raise objections, like many of us do. Every time God comes by with a new challenge, we say, "No, Lord, I can't."

Moses gave God all sorts of faults that prevented him from being the leader God was calling him to be. Let's look at the third of his eleven complaints.

> **And Moses answered and said, But, behold, they will not believe me, nor hearken unto my voice: for they will say, The Lord hath not appeared unto thee.**
>
> **And the Lord said unto him, What is that in thine hand?**
>
> **And he said, A rod.**
>
> **And He said, Cast it on the ground.**
>
> **And he cast it on the ground, and it became a serpent; and Moses fled from before it.**
>
> **And the Lord said unto Moses, Put forth thine hand, and take it by the tail.**
>
> **And he put forth his hand, and caught it, and it became a rod in his hand: That they may believe that the Lord, God of their fathers, the God of Abraham, the God of Isaac, and the God of Jacob, hath appeared unto thee.**
>
> **Exodus 4:1-5**

In essence, God said, "I've given you supernatural signs and wonders to prove to the people that I am with you."

Likewise, it's important for those you lead to see God's favor and empowerment operating in your life. They need to know that God is with you.

JOSHUA'S TURN

After Moses died, Joshua was left to finish what Moses started. I can imagine Joshua's response when God said to him, **Moses my**

servant is dead (Josh. 1:2). Joshua probably said, "Yeah, nobody knows that any better than me. I've got some big shoes to fill." But as Joshua assumed the position of leadership God had bestowed upon him, we see what the children of Israel said about the kind of leader they wanted:

> **And they answered Joshua, saying, All that thou commandest us we will do, and whithersoever thou sendest us, we will go. According as we hearkened unto Moses in all things, so will we hearken unto thee: only the Lord thy God be with thee, as he was with Moses.**
>
> **Joshua 1:16,17**

People have not changed from that time to today. Our technology and our environment have changed, but people's basic perceptions and values have not changed significantly. People want to see in a leader now what they wanted to see in a leader then.

DEFINED LEADERSHIP

Let's begin by defining leadership:

- LEADERSHIP IMPLIES THAT YOU HAVE THE CAPACITY OR ABILITY TO OBTAIN FOLLOWERS.
- LEADERSHIP IS A RELATIONAL SKILL.
- LEADERSHIP MODELS DESIRED BEHAVIORS.
- LEADERSHIP IS THE ABILITY TO ORGANIZE.

Now let's look at each of these one by one.

LEADERSHIP IMPLIES THAT YOU HAVE THE CAPACITY TO OBTAIN FOLLOWERS

If you think you are a leader, but nobody is following you, then you are not truly leading. Leadership implies that you exercise enough influence over other people so that they trust the direction you are taking and follow you in that direction.

LEADERSHIP IS A RELATIONAL SKILL

In order for you to influence people to follow your lead and in order to organize those people to pursue a common goal or objective, you must develop relational skills. A skill is not an aptitude you are born with; it is something you learn. It is not natural charisma. It is an acquired ability. And it is a vitally important one.

A Stanford University survey was taken by over 2000 of the most successful executives of this country—from the corporate world, the private entrepreneurial business arena and ministry. It demonstrated that 85 percent of the success of these executives was attributed to relational skills, not product knowledge. Plainly and simply put, their skill in developing, cultivating and conducting relationships is what makes them successful leaders.

Let's look at John 10 and focus on Jesus, our ultimate example of leadership.

> **But he that entereth in by the door** [Jesus] **is the shepherd of the sheep. To him the porter openeth; and the sheep hear his voice: and he calleth his own sheep by name, and leadeth them out. And when he putteth forth his own sheep, he goeth before them, and the sheep follow him: for they know his voice. And a stranger will they not follow, but will flee from him: for they know not the voice of strangers.**
>
> **John 10:2-5**

KNOWING YOUR SHEEP

Jesus knows His sheep, and His sheep know Him. There is an important leadership principle at the heart of this truth. The Word says so.

You cannot effectively lead unless you know the people you are leading and they know you. It is not enough for them to know you are in a position of authority. They must know *you*, and you must know *them*.

In particular, you must know well the people who are accountable to you. You must know inside and out how they think. You must know how they will respond to various circumstances. You must know their weaknesses and their strengths. You must know the areas in which they need support and encouragement. You must know what skills they have which can best be utilized to achieve the goal you desire.

As you establish relationships with people and they see in you those things they know they can trust, they will gain confidence in your leadership, and they will begin to follow you.

> *You must know well the people who are accountable to you. . . . You must know how they will respond to various circumstances.*

This is where failure begins for most leaders: Many people in leadership have the erroneous idea that their positional authority means they do not have to be totally honest with those whom they lead.

As leaders, we must be sure we do not have any hidden motives. Our agenda must be clear, not only to us but also to the people whom we serve. We must be transparent. We cannot say we feel one way when we feel another. We cannot profess loyalty to them and then demonstrate by our actions that we really do not care about them, that we only care about getting the job done. People are important, and they have to be made to feel important.

Mutual Familiarity

What John 10 is referring to, in modern terms, is mutual familiarity. And what that type of familiarity produces is trust. We see in those verses that those who follow the shepherd are not going to listen to any other voices. They know the voice of the one they are called to follow, and they are going to follow him. Why is that? Because through relationship, mutual familiarity, they know him and there is a basis for trusting his leadership.

Our relationships as leaders must produce that kind of trust.

You must be open in your communication. If someone does something you do not like or that is contrary to the direction you want to take, give them the benefit of the doubt. Say, "I know you didn't have a wrong motive; it was probably just a mistake. Let's figure out what happened and talk about it." That attitude will produce trust in your family, in your employees and in those laboring under your leadership. This will enable you to more effectively lead them.

THREE VITAL ATTRIBUTES

Be knowledgeable. This will only contribute to your credibility. You must be knowledgeable about the things of which you speak. You wouldn't want someone who has never flown an airplane to teach you how; you'd want a knowledgeable instructor. The same is true of those you lead.

The Word says to study to show yourself approved. (2 Tim. 2:15.) You are first approved by God through the blood of Jesus. But to be approved or accepted by men, you must study the Word, live by godly principles and receive and share right teaching with those whom you are called to lead. You cannot simply say, "Thus saith the Lord!" to cover up lapses in your knowledge base.

Be consistent. Employees who cannot predict what frame of mind their boss is going to be in will be reluctant to talk to him or her about anything. They won't know if that boss is going to bite their heads off or be polite; be sarcastic or genuine. But consistency in leadership is a key to engendering trust. After all, His perfect consistency is one of the reasons we can trust the Lord. He is the same yesterday, today, and forevermore. (Hebrews 13:8.)

We need consistency in leadership in order to build that same kind of trust.

Be responsible. Take ownership and responsibility for your own words. It confuses the issue when you say, "*We* don't think you should be doing what you're doing." Who is "we" anyway? The truth is that *you* don't think he should be doing what he is doing. Therefore, say, "I don't believe you are doing the right thing, and here's why." Take personal responsibility for how you share information.

So in the example of John 10, we see that leadership is a relational challenge. It begins by thoroughly knowing the people who work for you. That means spending time with them and talking to them, not just "directing traffic." Spend enough time with them to learn their hearts, their priorities and their values. You must know what turns them on and off and their strengths and weaknesses. Then let them get to know you; be transparent and consistent. The trust that you build will make you more effective in directing their activity and in leading them where they want to go.

Remember, Jesus did not direct from behind; He led from the front.

LEADERSHIP MODELS DESIRED BEHAVIORS

Effective leadership always models what you want from those who follow you. When you desire a specific result from those working for you, make sure it is being demonstrated in your own life. There is an impartation from you as a leader that will shape the way they act in their role. What they see in you is what they are going to become.

It is more than natural. It is supernatural. It involves the anointing of the Holy Spirit. God equips leadership with the anointing of the Spirit in order to bring direction to people's lives. If He elevates you to a position of responsibility in the body of Christ, you are anointed to impart direction to the people who follow you.

Model the attitudes, values and work ethic you want to see in your followers, and they *will* follow your lead. If you are walking the right way, your leadership will produce positive results in your followers.

Leadership Is the Ability To Organize

Leadership is an organized, managed effort to utilize all the human and natural resources entrusted to you. Organization enables you to accomplish God's purpose within the framework of your vision. Maybe your vision is to pursue full-time ministry, or maybe it is to grow a business or a city-wide volunteer effort.

Whatever it may be, launching that vision will require the human resources which have been entrusted to you—those who follow your lead. And you must organize those human resources along with material resources—knowledge, finances and so on—in order to achieve the desire the Lord has put in your heart.

Now that we've laid the basic groundwork of the principles of leadership, we can learn to develop that leadership gift God has bestowed on you.

```
┌─────┐
│  7  │
└─────┘
```

DEVELOPING AS A LEADER

God does not pluck you from the ranks and make you Number One overnight. Leadership is a progressive matter of individual development, and these principles are universal. They will work for corporations as well as the corporate body of Christ. But my framework, for our purposes, is ministry. In fact, there are five levels of leadership development.

THE STARTING PLACE

The Call. The first level of leadership is the call. Who is called to be a leader? How do you identify the call? Are you supposed to be a follower all your life and nothing more? A supervisor? Who is called to be a leader in the body of Christ?

As I pointed out in the opening chapter, since leadership is a matter of influencing the direction of another's life, then we are all called to be leaders. Each member of the body of Christ is called to influence the direction of another's life toward Jesus Christ, toward the plan of God, toward the Word of God.

That means that every one of us has an anointing to lead in some capacity. There is an anointing to lead on everyone who is born again. We are all called to be influencers of men.

God wants the body of Christ to lead this world into the millennial reign. God wants us to lead this world to Jesus Christ. He wants us to lead the unsaved into the knowledge of Him.

WHAT WILL YOU DO WITH THE ANOINTING YOU HAVE?

Being born again gives you the anointing to lead, to influence men. What you do with that anointing determines whether or not you go to the second level. Each level builds on the level which precedes it.

If someone who is born again does not use the anointing now available to them to influence other people for Jesus Christ, God cannot promote them in the kingdom. Certainly they will go to heaven. Their salvation will not be jeopardized or dependent on their stewardship of God's call to leadership. But as far as promotion to a higher level of influence, responsibility or leadership in the body of Christ, that will never happen.

God promotes faithfulness, and faithfulness requires us to do with our lives as He directs. If we are called and anointed to influence others for Him and we do not do it, we have not been faithful.

Influencing others for Jesus Christ is evangelism in its purest form. I know for some folks the word *evangelism* conjures up images of street witnessing and strikes fear in their hearts. They want no part of that. But influencing others for the Lord should not be viewed so narrowly. It simply means letting your light shine in accordance with your personality, your talents, your gifts, your social background, your acquaintances and your friends. You are unique, and when you let your light shine within the sphere of your influence, it will have a different result than when someone else lets his light shine.

Let the light shine! That may mean telling someone he needs Jesus. It may simply mean living by the values in God's Word and having someone notice it. It may be sharing the love of God with another person through an act of kindness.

There are a lot of ways in which we influence other people for Jesus Christ. But if we are not deliberate in our daily walk with God, consciously pursuing opportunities to influence others, we may occasionally open the door for conversation but be counted unfaithful because we do not press through and truly influence them for Jesus Christ.

If we are not faithful to use the anointing to affect another's life for Him, we will not be promoted in the Kingdom of God to a higher level of leadership.

If you are faithful to use the anointing He entrusts to you to influence people for Him, God will give you a position of authority.

After the call comes the second level of developing leadership, Position.

Position. Your new position of leadership could be anything from leading a Bible study or home care group to a supervisory opportunity at work. It is a position of some leadership responsibility that is officially recognized. At this level, you have received "positional authority."

The danger of positional authority is that the leader may come to rely on having people follow him solely because of his position.

This type of person says, "Do what I say because I'm in charge, not because of who I am or the relationship we have. Don't you forget who's boss around here." If that is the attitude you adopt, you will never move beyond this second level of leadership.

For example, I've seen a hard-working, front-line employee promoted to a management position because of his diligence. At this point, he has no experience; he only has the position. He walks into the workplace and assumes that everyone is going to follow him just because he is the boss. It usually takes about a year and you find that guy packing his U-Haul and leaving.

Positional authority, or the idea that someone will follow your lead because they have to, is one of the most ill-conceived ideas about leadership there is. And yet it's also one of the most common reasons leaders fail.

"SIR, YES SIR!"

Leadership was once all positional for me, because of my background in the military. I almost made it my career. I went to a military academy, went into Air Force pilot training and flew for six years. The military was my background, so everything I understood about leadership at that point in my life was positional.

I had to salute anyone who was an officer because they had a position. The captain, the major, the lieutenant colonel, the wing commander, the colonel—whoever. They were leaders because of their rank. Their position of authority made them a leader in my estimation.

But even in the military it did not take long for me to recognize a certain truth: Leadership is not purely positional. I discovered that there were men who had the rank, but nobody would have followed them to a dogfight. Yet there were other men, often of lesser rank, who commanded such respect that others often sought to follow after them.

I began to realize that true leadership is not altogether positional.

There was another element involved which the Lord has helped me identify in recent years. For someone to succeed in leadership, he must first realize that it is a relational undertaking. Leadership is not about position; leadership is about relationships.

Secondly, your ability to relate effectively is cultivated. It does not have anything to do with your personality, nor does it have anything to do with how naturally charismatic you are. There is no such thing as a born leader—you have to be taught how to lead.

Relationship. The third level of leadership is the Relationship level. This is the one in which people follow you, not because they have to, but because they want to.

This is the level at which they will do more for you than the job description requires. Why? Because they want to please you. This is where leadership truly begins to be effective. This is where it begins to be fun. People want to follow your lead because you have done what is necessary to cultivate a relationship with them that makes them want to follow you.

> *A good question to ask yourself as you anticipate this level is: What qualities in people makes me want to follow them?*

A good question to ask yourself as you anticipate this level is: What qualities in people makes me want to follow them? Think of someone you consider a good leader. Decide what you believe has made him or her effective. Then develop those qualities or traits in your own life.

In many respects, we are all the same. We do not like dishonesty. We do not like subterfuge. We do not like manipulation. We do not like arrogance. We do not like haughtiness. We do not like prideful people who impose their will upon us. We do not like to do things which do not make sense.

A lot of leaders say, "You don't need to know why you have to do this. I don't have time to tell you why. Just do it." Well, you can get away with that for a while, and there may be occasions, such as an emergency situation, when that is a legitimate thing to say. But for the most part, people need to know that what they are doing makes sense. So when you give direction to people, ask yourself the question, "Am I giving them sufficient reason to follow me?"

I want a leader to have integrity. I want him to be faithful to his word. I want him to be loyal to me. I want him to be open and honest.

I want to know he cares about me. I want to know he is bringing the same qualities to the relationship that he is asking me to bring.

Why do you think we follow Jesus? We know He cares about us. He has our best interests at heart. As a leader, you too must have your followers' best interests at heart.

The Fruit. The fourth level of leadership is the one I call the fruit. The purpose of effective leadership is to accomplish something, to achieve the results you desire. At the end of the day, you must produce results, or fruit.

In the long run, people will follow you not only because you have the position, not only because they want to, but because they see their efforts producing results.

Your followers need to see the fruit of their labor; they need to see themselves achieving their goals. Their accomplishments will light a fire in them that will feed their desire to accomplish even more. This is an exciting level of leadership. This is the level at which explosive growth most often occurs.

I have seen many churches, ministries and business organizations at this stage of their development. When you look at a graph of their growth, it is rarely a straight profile. When the people making the effort begin to see results, there is a flurry of phenomenal growth for maybe a year or so. This really is one of the most exciting levels of leadership.

Then the activity can seem too slow, or maybe even cease for two, three or even four years. Everything can seem static when, in fact, things have not really remained static at all. The organization has simply been consolidating past growth and preparing for the next push. New relationships have to be cultivated. The next level of goals and objectives has to be communicated. Then all of a sudden, there is another growth spurt and the graph goes up again.

When you have invested in relationships and they have developed properly and when people are following because they want to, the result is like setting a lit match to kindling. It sets flame to the activity within the organization.

When you have tangible, visible results, people want to be a part of that, and they are more on fire than they have ever been before.

But if you do not produce fruit, you will lose the people who have a vision for their lives and for what they want to see accomplished. (And these are precisely the people you want to hang on to!) It does not matter how much they like you—if they do not see results, they will eventually move on.

But even after results are achieved and the fruit becomes apparent, if you stop there, you can still limit growth, because there is only so much you and your leadership team can do unless you also develop leadership skills in those following you.

Reproduction. I call the fifth and highest level of leadership the reproduction. The highest level of leadership is when you recognize and deliberately cultivate leadership qualities in the people following you, preparing them to assume a role of leadership in the organization. When you begin developing leaders under you, this is where long-range growth occurs.

Let's say you are in charge of the direct-mail department of an organization. You have a dozen employees, and you are trying to plan for some anticipated growth within your department.

Too much of the time our mentality is, "We'll hire the people we need when the growth comes. Once we get busy we'll go out and find the leaders or get the managers or supervisors." This is a mistake. God is not going to expand you to a point where you cannot manage the growth He brings. That would be poor management on His part.

You must prepare for the growth before it comes. The preparation is made by developing leaders within the department as you continue to develop as the leader of the department. When you begin to reproduce yourself as a leader in those under you, preparing them for a role of leadership, then you have ascended to level number five.

WHY PEOPLE FOLLOW

Each of these levels helps us understand why people follow.

1. When you respond to the anointing to influence another, you have answered the call.

2. When others follow because they have to, you have moved to the positional level.

3. When others follow because they want to, you have moved to the relational level.

4. When others see tangible results as a function of your leadership, you have achieved the fruit level.

5. When others are growing and developing as leaders themselves, you have achieved the reproductive level.

At this point, you have the deepest kind of loyalty established within an organization. You have loyalties so strong that the Devil cannot divide them. When all of these levels are in place, you have an organization primed for long-term growth, primed to continue through all the storms the enemy can whip up, because these loyalties come only as a result of having moved through all five levels of leadership development. What level are you on?

8

LOOKING DEEPER

Let me make a few observations about the leadership levels I have just described.

We are all called to a place of leadership, so the positional level of leadership is really the entry level. This position is typically based on title, not talent or ability. Therefore, it is extremely limited. It has no safety net. If you lose your title, you will lose your following. If you do not move on from the positional level, there is no place of authority to fall back on. You simply return to the general ranks from which you were raised in the first place.

Very little can be accomplished on the positional level. If you remain on this level, you will experience great turnover. People are not going to serve for any length of time under someone they are forced to follow but do not want to serve.

A lot of turnover is one indication that you are on the positional level and are not moving up. You will not be able to keep people.

Another indication that you have remained on this level is hearing a lot of grumbling and griping. The Bible calls it strife and division. How often have you heard these words: "Those rebellious people in my department don't understand God's order of authority! I'm sent to this office. I'm anointed to stand here. Look at them. They're touching God's anointed." That is the cry of someone trying to promote his own agenda from the most basic level of authority. The result will be turnover, strife and division. Until that leader changes his attitude, he will never go any further.

THE FUN LEVEL

The relationship level is the fun level because everybody likes to be liked. At this level you are leading because people respond willingly to the direction they are given. You have done the things necessary to cultivate those relationships. You have gained their trust, a measure of their respect, and they want to follow you. You have been open and transparent with them. You have let them know you care about them, you love them, and you want them to be happy. You have done the things which make them want to follow your lead. All these factors make this the fun level.

And this is the level where you will begin to get extra effort from those who are working for you. They won't perform simply within their job description. One of the earmarks of your move up to the relationship level is that, as the need arises, those under you will willingly put in extra time. They will go beyond what is required in order to fulfill the direction you bring to them. So it is vital that you give attention to cultivating the relationships which will bring you to this point.

Still, I have seen managers who are really good at cultivating relationships, yet they never produce any results. They are charismatic leaders; everybody likes them. But they reach a certain point of growth or ministry development and level off because they do not develop the kind of organization which will produce results. Consequently, they never grow. Their growth curve levels off pretty early because the people get discouraged at the lack of fruitfulness. Eventually, they will have to start over.

THE PLATEAU PROBLEM

As a pastor, I have discovered that I can know only about 250 to 300 people in my church really well. I can remember their names, and I know their families and their backgrounds. But past that, I start getting a little confused. It is too difficult for anyone to really know more than a few hundred people in any meaningful sense.

A lot of churches grow initially, then level off somewhere between 100 and 200 people. They have a charismatic leader, and the folks like him. They want to follow his lead, but organizationally he does not know how to build a foundation for growth. He does not know how to communicate his vision, set goals and objectives or manage by those objectives. He does not know the basic principles which provide for more growth, so he stops growing. He loses the potential producers from his congregation, the ones who like him and want to serve under him, but are driven by result-oriented activity.

You see, that is part of the way we are made. Most people want to see results; they want to know that what they are doing is producing good results.

So people who are well-equipped educationally or spiritually to do big things within that ministry tend to go somewhere else because the direction that is needed is not coming. Eventually the ministry will consist of complacent people who are happy coming to church once every other week or so, people who aren't concerned about results. The congregation will dwindle to a number the pastor can handle. I call this "growing a church down to a level a pastor can manage," the sign of not graduating from the relational, or fun, level.

This principle applies to businesses as well as churches.

BIG "MO"

"Momentum" is a popularized concept for entrepreneurs, political leaders and sports figures. More and more, its value is being recognized.

Momentum is defined as an impulse or a driving force which feeds upon itself. In other words, the success that you realize is involved with generating your next success.

You can see momentum at work in the presidential campaign of 1992. It is my personal belief that incumbent George Bush lost the campaign to Bill Clinton because he could not sustain any momentum. I believe he had more people agreeing with his proposed policies than Bill Clinton did. But in spite of popular support, Bush could never generate enough groundswell of momentum to carry him to victory. So he lost.

Momentum must be a fact of life if success is to result. If you are talented or diligent and hard-working, without momentum, you can experience success only on a sporadic basis. But momentum fosters consistent success rather than occasional victory. It is momentum that carries you from one victory to another, from one success to another. It is momentum that gives you the ability to sustain repetitive successes and ultimately achieve the long-range goals you have set.

MAXWELL'S MAXIMS

There is a lot of teaching about momentum right now. A lot of it is secular. But there is a man, well-known in the body of Christ, whose teaching on momentum is excellent. His name is John Maxwell. In his book, *The 21 Irrefutable Laws of Leadership*, Maxwell has made some critical observations about momentum which will give you an appreciation for the concept and its value as well as its critical importance to your ministry's success.

"Many times momentum is the only difference between winning or losing," he says. There may be somebody who has great skill, talent and ability, wonderful ideas and is a good communicator, but he still doesn't win.

Let's take a look at some other of Maxwell's maxims: "With momentum, leaders look better than they really are. When you're on a roll, when you're winning and things are going your way, you look mighty good."

"With momentum, followers perform better." They in fact perform on a much higher level than they normally would. They produce more fruit.

"Without momentum, leaders look worse than they really are."

> *"If you have momentum going for you, you can make mistakes and the people that you're leading will forgive you very quickly. It won't be a big issue. . . ."*

I heard another man make this comment: "If you have momentum going for you, you can make mistakes and the people that you're leading will forgive you very quickly. It won't be a big issue. Without momentum, you make mistakes and they never forget and seldom forgive."

Momentum is the greatest of all change agents, according to Maxwell.

"It's easier to stir momentum than start it," he advises, so be very conscious of not killing it once you have it.

Maxwell lists the following as earmarks of an organization which has momentum:

- Expectancy
- High morale and good attitude
- High energy for getting projects completed

- High commitment level
- Confidence in the leadership[1]

NO MO, NO GO

On the contrary, in organizations where momentum is absent you will find doubt in the leader's ability. The decisions he makes are often questioned. That uncertainty produces procrastination at times when important decisions must be made. Decisions are not made in a timely fashion because the leader does not want to expose himself to any more criticism or doubt in his ability. Oftentimes decisions are avoided altogether.

Risks are rarely taken in an organization where there is no momentum. You have to be willing to risk some things to make progress in the Kingdom of God. I'm not talking about foolish or haphazard risks. I am talking about risks which may seem to carry a natural, negative consequence; but after prayer, you are confident the Lord has led you in that direction.

Oftentimes, there comes a devotion to false symbols. This is how a religious spirit can enter in. In other words, when we do not have momentum to achieve the things that are really in our heart, we lift up ritualistic practices or things which have no value, focusing our attention upon them. Because we are not making progress toward our goals, we raise these false icons in our ministries and in our lives.

Without momentum, complacency is always in evidence. Loss of purpose is always in evidence. The goal becomes to maintain the status quo.

These characteristics are quite a contrast from the organizations in which there is a high energy level, an expectancy of good things to come, confidence in the leadership, depth of commitment and human and financial resources available to get the job done. And the only difference is momentum.

GOOD NEWS

The good news is that we can learn some basics about generating momentum that will enable us to become effective leaders. Maxwell makes the observation that there is a formula to help generate momentum in an organization. And there are three major contributing factors: The attitude of the leader, the atmosphere of the organization and the experience of success among the people, the corporate body.

These are the three principle ingredients in momentum. If we can generate the right kind of attitude in the leadership, if we can generate the right kind of atmosphere in our church or in our organization and if we can begin to experience some success, momentum will result.

What attitude is right? What kind of organizational atmosphere do we want to generate? And what about success?

The book of Joshua gives one of the most dramatic accounts of sustained success that any group of people has ever experienced. After their one defeat at Ai, Israel had a string of twenty-eight consecutive victories.

Joshua knew about momentum, so in the next chapter let's take a look at his example.

9

ATTITUDES AND ACTIONS

It came to pass, when Moses went out unto the tabernacle, that all the people rose up, and stood every man at his tent door, and looked after Moses, until he was gone into the tabernacle. And it came to pass, as Moses entered into the tabernacle, the cloudy pillar descended, and stood at the door of the tabernacle, and the Lord talked with Moses.

And all the people saw the cloudy pillar stand at the tabernacle door: and all the people rose up and worshipped, every man in his tent door.

And the Lord spake unto Moses face to face, as a man speaketh unto his friend. And he turned again into the camp: but his servant Joshua, the son of Nun, a young man, departed not out of the tabernacle.

Exodus 33:8-11

Momentum is born in prayer. A lot of times we rely on the things we do naturally to generate excitement or activity in our churches or our groups. But prayer is how God imparts the vision, and it is the birth-place of momentum.

THE LEADER'S ATTITUDE

The first thing we see about Joshua is that he **departed not out of the tabernacle** (v. 11). He was a seeker of God who gave himself to prayer. This is how God birthed the vision to direct and propel him into the Land of Promise. That same place of prayer will also reveal the will of God for our lives and for our ministries.

There is a Canaan Land for everyone. It is a land of promise which flows with milk and honey. It is a good place. It is a good land in which you will be blessed and happy and effective. But there are giants in the land. There are walled cities. There are obstacles to your moving into that Land of Promise. You must have clear vision, direction and momentum to move into the will of God for your life. And it is all born in prayer.

Long before Joshua assumed the leadership of the nation of Israel, the book of Numbers records that he was one of the twelve spies Moses sent to spy out the land. He was one of two who came back with a good report. Yes, there were giants in the land. Yes, there were obstacles. But Joshua and Caleb, the spies with a good report, chose to look on the good things, not the obstacles or the giants, and they brought a good report.

"We can take the land. We can do it," they said. (Num. 13:30.)

The other ten spies brought an evil report. They said, "No, we can't. There are fortified cities. There are giants, and we are as grasshoppers in their sight." (Num. 13:31-33.) And the Bible says their evil report did something to the people's hearts. It "melted" their hearts.

MELTED HEARTS

That is how leaders kill momentum, let it die or, worse yet, never let it be born—they melt the hearts of the people by focusing on the obstacles instead of the promise. We all have challenges, whether it is a new building, a contrary city council or a disagreeable coworker. No matter what they may be, we all have obstacles. Be sure, as a leader, that you do not lift up the obstacles before the people because, as the Bible says, it will melt their hearts.

The attitude of a leader must inspire confidence, confidence in the people to accomplish the task before them and confidence in your leadership to take them where they want to go. What is it that makes a person confident in your leadership? Confidence in *yourself*.

You can declare until you are purple in the face that you are the pastor and they have to do what you say. But momentum will never occur until you inspire confidence in the people you are leading.

You must be a seeker of God, and your followers must see that in you. You cannot just talk about it. They have to see your heart for God. They also have to know you spend time seeking Him in your own life. They have to know it is your priority.

SHOULDERED RESPONSIBILITY

Effective leadership conveys the knowledge that a person has accepted responsibility for the success or failure of a ministry or organization.

Joshua never said, "Well, it's so-and-so's fault," or, "We can't do this because I don't have the human resources we need." Joshua accepted the responsibility of leadership.

Stop blaming other people. It doesn't matter whether or not it is your congregation, people who minister to you or others in the body of Christ; your success or failure as a leader is your responsibility.

"Well, they're lucky and I'm not."

Sorry.

"They're in the right place and I'm not."

Too bad.

"I don't have any big givers in my church."

Sell that down the block!

Your success is *your* responsibility.

Joshua never shifted blame to anyone else. Moses used to talk about this bunch of people God had given him. He would get frustrated and say, "Kill 'em, God, and do us both a favor!" But Joshua never did. One time he slipped at Ai after Israel's defeat because of sin in the camp. (Josh. 7:7.) But once the Lord told Joshua what the problem was, he never again said the nation's problems were because of her people. He always accepted the responsibility.

So be a seeker of God. Accept responsibility for your ministry's success and momentum toward success. And let the people know that you have accepted that responsibility. You do not have to get up and make an announcement because your followers will see in your attitude whether you are taking responsibility for what is happening or not.

Knowledge Builds Confidence

Be knowledgeable about every aspect of your ministry. People can tell when you are trying to cover up for a lack of information. If you do not know what is going on in your ministry, people will notice. Do you think people will be confident in your leadership if they know you always have to check with someone else before you can make a decision? You do not have to know everything, but you must have a grasp of the big picture. You must know what is going on, so stay current.

Decisions, Decisions

Be decisive. Joshua did not have any problem making decisions. Israel made a move toward the Land of Promise before the River Jordan ever parted. Joshua made a decision and moved on the basis of that decision. The waters did not part until the priest's foot got wet. (Josh. 3.)

Now, there is always a need to draw on the wisdom of peers, and pray and then be decisive. Oftentimes, however, the tendency is to wait until everything is just perfect and then make a decision. If Joshua had waited for the water to part, he would still be standing on the other side!

Any decision is better than no decision. God can correct a moving ship; He cannot correct one that is "dead in the water."

Be willing to take risks. Folks do not want a Milquetoast leader who is afraid to step out and take a risk to do something for God. Seek God, trust God and then do it.

> *Any decision is better than no decision. God can correct a moving ship; He cannot correct one that is "dead in the water."*

The attitude of the leader has an enormous effect on the momentum and the motivation of the workers who are under his direction. That attitude has to be a "can do" attitude, not born out of mindless optimism, but based on the Scripture which says you can do all things through Christ who strengthens you. (Phil. 4:13.)

There is no reason to accept any situation as unmanageable. There is absolutely nothing beyond your capability or reach. You can do it all through Christ. You must know that. And the people who follow you must know that too.

GOD-BREATHED ENTHUSIASM

Be enthusiastic. Your attitude must be more than positive; it must be enthusiastic. If you are not enthusiastic about what you are doing, how are you going to fire up those who are following you so they will be motivated to give an extra measure of effort?

Artificial enthusiasm is as transparent as a cheap shirt, and it will not produce any results. You must be genuinely enthusiastic about what you are doing. If you aren't and if spending time meditating on what lies before you does not generate that kind of enthusiasm, you may be in the wrong place.

There are some pitfalls that can sap your enthusiasm, such as stress, strife or not enough time with God. But if you spend a little time each day during your private devotions praying in the Spirit and allowing Him to continually paint the dream on your heart and stir you up, you will go to work fired up and genuinely enthusiastic.

Every January, when our church seeks God for the New Year's vision, I always get up and say the same thing: "This is the most dynamite year we are ever going to have."

Someone once said to me, "You say that every year. You have said that every year for ten years." But it's true. And that is the way I feel. I feel each year that it will to be the best year. You see, I cannot light a fire in your heart if it does not burn in mine.

STOKING THE FIRES OF ENTHUSIASM

I realize there are times in everyone's life and ministry when being enthusiastic is not your first choice. It is difficult to be enthusiastic when you are facing a bad report or a challenge that intimidates you. But enthusiasm is a decision you make. It is not based on how you feel; it is based on the exceeding, precious promises of God.

Make the decision right now that you are going to be enthusiastic, that the fire is going to burn in you, no matter what happens. You have to be excited—more excited about what God is doing right now than you have ever been. Otherwise, you can forget about generating momentum or inspiring confidence in your leadership.

If you look hang-dog about what is going on and your attitude is "Well, we have this huge challenge, folks. They're going to turn off the utilities if we don't get enough money in the offering today," just forget it! Go sell shoes or something. You have to be enthusiastic no matter what the circumstance is. I am not talking about pretending to be enthusiastic. People can see through that. It has to come from the heart.

This is part of stirring yourself up. You have to stir yourself up about the vision God has placed in your heart. You have to see it so clearly that you can impart your enthusiasm to other people. They have to see you excited about what is going on. Because, friend, without enthusiasm, you will never inspire anyone to follow you, you will never inspire confidence in your leadership, you will never generate momentum.

Don't wait on God to drop a little glory cloud on your congregation or your organization. Get into your prayer closet and stay there until you have a flame in your spirit that you can fan into a blaze. Then make something happen.

DANCE, DANCE, DANCE

On several occasions, I've heard Brother Kenneth Hagin say, "You may start out dancing in the flesh, but then the Spirit of God falls on you." What he means is that if nothing is happening in your organization, make something happen. I'm not getting carnal about this. I have more reverence and respect for genuine moves of the Holy Spirit than I have ever had in my life. But I know that as a leader, you cannot allow inertia to set in.

Invest your resources in those things or people who have demonstrated their ability to generate momentum. God will raise up people in your organization who have the ability to get things moving. Excitement follows them, so invest your resources in them. Put them on staff. Support their efforts. Give them what they need. Do not become jealous of their gifts. God gave them to you because you need help in that area. Cultivate them. Direct them.

Remove the fear of failure from your people. One of the greatest momentum killers is a fear of failure. If, as a leader, you have criticized people who have made mistakes, you will eventually intimidate them to a point that they are afraid to step out.

Let people know you support them. Say, "Hey, taking a risk means occasional failure. Sometimes we miss it. But the world isn't going to end there. God's in the business of restoration, is He not? And if our motivation and our hearts are right, we are promoting His interests to the best of our ability. If we miss it and fail, so what!" If I fall, I shall arise. (Prov. 24:16.) Get up and try it again!

If they experience some failure, let them know that in your eyes their credibility has not suffered a bit. Neither will their paycheck. Neither will their job security. Eliminate the fear of failure by making sure your followers understand that occasional failure is not a problem for you. Encourage them to be as determined as they can possibly be, regardless of the outcome.

Celebrate victories. One thing you see consistently in the lives of the children of Israel is they knew how to celebrate a victory. They made it a big occasion. We should learn how to make big occasions out of our victories—even ones that seem relatively small. In church, we ask someone to testify about God's goodness, and then praise Him for it, letting the rafters shake.

Israel even built memorials, for example, when they crossed the River Jordan. They built a rock memorial, a pile of stones, at Gilgal. And why did they do that? It was to be a monument to their success so generations of children after them would know God had worked a miracle.

Their celebration was not just a two- or three-minute affair on Sunday morning: sing an extra chorus and give God a handclap. Their victories included building monuments to God's faithfulness so even their children would be able to share in the glorious testimony of what God had done.

10

ENVIRONMENT AND SUCCESS

The Bible makes it clear: the environment or the atmosphere which surrounds any organizational effort, has to be one where everyone is striving together for the faith of the gospel. (Phil. 1:27.) There can be no room for personal agendas or any kind of divisive individualism. If momentum is ever going to develop, there has to be unity, singleness of purpose, oneness in goal and objective—in other words, momentum develops when people are striving together for the faith of the gospel.

The Bible asks how two can possibly walk together "except they be agreed." (Amos 3:3.) That does not mean we are always going to share the same opinion; but at minimum, there ought to be the kind of dialog which promotes new ideas and creative thought and generates new ways of doing things.

The Hebrew word translated *agreed* in Amos 3:3 means "concord and harmony."[1] How can two walk together except there be concord and harmony and singleness of purpose, unless they be striving together for the faith of the gospel?

The popular idea in much of our secular world today is "Do your own thing. Focus on your agenda or your career. If your thing isn't getting tended to, you can always go on strike."

You go to work at some places and it seems as though no one cares; everyone is just putting in their time: "Here we are for another day." There might be a little strife and division over here, Mary Jane is complaining about her boss doing this or not doing that over there and someone else is griping about something else.

Saint of God, there is no room in an organization for any kind of divisive influence if that organization is going to do what God has called it to do.

NIPPING STRIFE

As a leader, you cannot allow one tiny inch's worth of strife to develop in those following you. Nip it in the bud when it rears its head; deal with it right then. Sit down with the parties involved in the divisiveness or strife and say, "Hey! We can't let this happen. I understand you have a concern about this or that or you feel this or that didn't go well. That's fine. Let's talk about it and work it out.

"You need to understand that the Bible says this is something we cannot allow. We cannot allow this kind of divisiveness to occur in this organization. We have to deal with it. And if this has produced such a deep-seated resentment in you that you cannot settle this issue in your heart, you're going to have to find another place to work. I hope that's not the case. I want to address your concern, but you need to understand that there is nothing worth our allowing this kind of influence to remain. You're going to have to deal with it."

The atmosphere that enables momentum to happen is one in which everyone is pulling together: having singleness of heart, singleness of mind, striving together for a common vision.

We can do whatever needs to be done. We can do it because the Bible says we can. It may be a challenge to our flesh, but we can do all things through Christ. (Phil. 4:11.) That kind of attitude creates the atmosphere needed for the organization to stay alive and thrive.

There will be times when you do not meet a goal or an objective. There will be occasions when failure does occur. Don't hide it, but do not make it a focus of everyone's attention. Minimize the publicity of failure, and maximize the publicity of victory. The kind of atmosphere you generate has to be one of victory–consciousness, not failure–consciousness.

> *"Yes, we've been talking about pulling together, striving together. . . Look what happened. Look at the results we are getting!"*

SEEING RESULTS

When people see the results of their efforts, it is like kindling a match. Begin saying, "Yes, we've been talking about pulling together, striving together. He's been saying we can do it, and now we know we can. Look what happened. Look at the results we are getting!"

The ball starts rolling, and this supernatural thing called momentum begins to occur. It is a supernatural thing because when momentum is generated it seems that everything just works better. Morale is high, and turnover is low. Needs are met, goals are realized and problems are solved when momentum is part of the ministry thrust.

JUGGLING THE MANDATE OF GOD

Let's look at the one occasion when Joshua did experience failure and see why the failure came and what he did to keep it from robbing him of his momentum. In fact, Joshua used the lesson of his failure to launch him into twenty-eight consecutive victories.

Prior to the battle of Jericho in Joshua 6, the Captain of the Lord's hosts, Jesus, appeared to Joshua and gave him the strategy for winning the city. In that instruction He had something to say about the spoil.

And the city shall be accursed, even it and all that are therein, to the Lord: only Rahab the harlot shall live, she and all that are with her in the house, because she hid the messengers that we sent.

And ye, in any wise keep yourselves from the accursed thing, lest ye make yourselves accursed, when ye take of the accursed thing, and make the camp of Israel a curse, and trouble it.

Joshua 6:17,18

Scripture says the city shall be accursed, the Hebrew word is *cherem*. This word literally means "consecrated or devoted to the Lord."[2] And the instruction of the Captain of the Lord's host to Joshua was, "Don't take anything from this city. This city is consecrated to the Lord. It is devoted to God."

Now, there was a man named Achan who took certain treasures from the city after Jericho fell. **But the children of Israel committed a trespass in the accursed thing: for Achan, the son of Carmi...of the tribe of Judah, took of the accursed thing: and the anger of the Lord was kindled against the children of Israel** (Josh. 7:1).

THE RESULTS

Jericho was a huge city with 750,000 inhabitants, surrounded by a wall thick enough to have chariot races on the top. The next little city, Ai, had 12,000 people. It was merely a drop in the bucket compared to the odds Israel had just faced. But when Joshua tried to conquer Ai, he and his men were soundly defeated!

Here was the crucial point for Joshua as a leader. He could lose all the momentum which had been generated by the great victory at

Jericho, or he could deal with the problem in a way which would sustain momentum in the long run. This is what happened.

In a sense, you can say it is human nature that we sometimes do not take the mandate of God seriously. God said, "Don't touch anything in the city. It is all Mine." Achan heard it. He knew it. But he did it anyway.

How many occasions have we known exactly what the mandate of God was, but to accommodate our own agendas or desires—our flesh—we have juggled that mandate? Ministries juggle in a lot of ways. For example, some supposedly full-gospel churches have said, "Well, the baptism in the Holy Spirit and speaking in tongues is a pretty dicey subject. We are just not going to make that a real centerpiece of our ministry. We don't want to scare anybody away." What are they doing? They are juggling the mandate of God.

We juggle in a lot of ways to accommodate our own insecurities, our own agendas, our own flesh. We juggle socially and say, "Well, you know, a lot of young people experiment sexually before marriage. Anyway, how can you really know you're compatible with someone if you don't sleep with that person?"

We juggle the life right out of a woman's womb with abortion and call it a choice. We juggle the mandate of God and wonder why the curse comes.

ACHAN'S PARTICULAR SIN

But the particular sin here is important, too, because this, more than anything else, speaks of a ministry's heart. God said not to touch the accursed thing. Everything was consecrated to the Lord. Why was it consecrated to the Lord? What was so special about Jericho?

When you study this Hebrew word *cherem*, "consecrated or devoted to the Lord," you find it also used in the book of Leviticus regarding the tithe. Leviticus 27:28-30 says the tithe is consecrated and wholly devoted to the Lord. In Malachi 3:9, a curse is pronounced if the tithe is withheld. "Devoted to the Lord" means it is serious business.

Remember, Jericho was Israel's first victory in the Land of Promise. It was the firstfruits of conquest in a land Israel was to occupy as its own. Never again did God say, "Save the spoils for Me." In every other battle from then on they could take whatever they wanted. Jericho was the only time God said, "It is devoted to Me. Don't touch it."

TOMORROW'S VICTORIES

Tomorrow's victory depends upon giving God our firstfruits today. If you fail to give God the firstfruits, then there will never be any momentum in your efforts. How do you give God the firstfruits? Through your giving. You need to be involved in supporting churches and ministries.

Which ones? The fathers of your faith! Just as Paul told the church at Corinth, **For though ye have ten thousand instructors in Christ, yet have ye not many fathers: for in Christ Jesus I have begotten you through the gospel. Wherefore I beseech you, be ye followers of me** (1 Cor. 4:15,16).

Later he said, "Hey, I planted this vineyard. It's not wrong of me to partake of the fruit. We've given you spiritual things. We need to receive from you carnal things." (1 Cor. 9:9-11.)

Give God the firstfruits of your efforts. Give it to those who are the fathers of your faith, those who have planted the seed and who have watered the seed that has caused you to grow spiritually.

In a general sense, what stopped Joshua's momentum was the violation of the principle of the firstfruits. Similarly, our victory tomorrow depends on our giving God the firstfruits today.

Victory From the Jaws of Defeat

But Joshua turned his failure around. How? By not sweeping the problem under the rug. He assumed responsibility for it. He repented and then he took care of the problem.

We could look at the example of Achan and say, "Man, that's harsh! They dragged him and his whole family out and all of his cattle, his sheep, everything he had and they killed them. Dead! They stoned them and then burned them. That's tough. Poor ol' Achan got the raw end of that deal, didn't he?" No. Achan represents our tendency to treat the mandate of God casually, our tendency to interpret God's direction for our lives in light of what we want instead of what God has said we're to do.

Our tendency is to compromise. Our tendency is to be complacent toward the things God has directed us to do and to make little alterations here or there as we deem necessary. And God is saying, "Kill it," because it will kill momentum. It will kill success.

You have to walk the straight and narrow. You have to be as deliberate as you can be in following the direction of the Lord—both the written direction of His Word and the revealed direction of the Holy Spirit—for your life.

When something in your organization threatens your momentum, do the same thing Joshua did. He made it a public affair in front of his whole following. "We blew it. We made a mistake. And we're going to eradicate this problem forever," he said. Don't try to sweep your mistakes under the rug. When you have made a mistake, come clean.

I am not suggesting you lay out in front of your organization every little thing you have ever done wrong. That's not wisdom. But when you have made a mistake that has affected the progress of the group, then you have to be as deliberate in dealing with it as Joshua was. You have to stand before your people and say, "This is what happened. I take responsibility for it. It has created problems for us as a whole, and here is what we are going to do to change it, right now, today." The result for

Joshua was that he got back on track. Momentum was restored, and Israel won twenty-eight consecutive victories!

Taking responsibility for and eradicating problems as they arise affects the momentum of your organization. And momentum has everything to do with your success.

SECTION 2

The Leadership Vision

11

LEADERSHIP FOCUS

As you know, you cannot change the quality of your life without first accepting responsibility for your life. You are not where you are because of the color of your skin or because you were born to a poor family or into a compromised socioeconomic condition. The quality of the life you are experiencing isn't less than it could be because your boss does not like you, because you do not have a degree or because you have never had an opportunity to be mentored.

These are all things which may give another person an edge in the natural, but as far as God is concerned, they make absolutely no difference. Why? Because the way He has prepared for us to experience success relies upon none of these things.

The first thing you have to do is stop saying, "I'm like I am because of my color, because of where I was born, because of my background or because I don't have the education." That has to stop right now.

If you're not where you want to be, you have to learn to say, "I am where I am because I have not applied very well the principles which govern prosperity. God has provided the direction I need to experience success. That direction is found in His laws of prosperity. I'll just have to dig deeper until I find the key."

When God says in 3 John 2, **Beloved, I wish above all things that thou mayest prosper and be in health, even as thy soul prospereth**, He is not only talking about your physical health; He is referring to every aspect of your life. He wants you to prosper spiritually, of course. Soulishly, in your mind, your will and your emotions, physically and financially. God wants you totally blessed.

GOD'S WILL FOR YOUR LIFE

If Adam had not sinned, we would still be living in a blessed paradise. That was God's will then, and it is God's will for your life in Jesus now. The Bible is God's instruction manual for living that blessed, higher quality of life. That kind of life is called zoe life.[1]

When Jesus said, **I am...the life** (John 14:6), He was referring to this zoe life—the God kind of life—a quality of life that makes no room for sickness, disease, poverty or any other accursed thing. Then why don't you have it? Well, God is not a liar, so it must be that you do not completely understand how His laws work.

But change comes only when people realize they can have a positive effect on their own lives. As long as they are finding excuses for why they are like they are, they will never change.

It's the same in business. Don't tell anyone, "Well, I haven't experienced the success I want because of these people. This is such a small town. They're just knotheads. They won't get committed."

Let me tell you something, friend. The laws work for you and your business just as well as they work for any individual. If you are not prospering, increasing or growing in the way that you want to prosper, increase or grow, the problem is sitting right in your chair.

You have to face that. I am not trying to be offensive, but if you do not change, your results will not change. If you do not address the truth of your own shortcomings, God cannot do anything to correct them.

THE APPLICATION

If that has jolted you awake a little bit, good. God not only wants you restored to Him spiritually, He wants you to be healed physically. He wants you to have good relationships. He wants your light to shine. He wants you to have something that is attractive to the rest of the world. They don't need poverty or sickness; they need to see the light of your health and prosperity.

God wants the same for your career, business or ministry. You are going to attract people when you are successfully applying the laws that govern the blessings of God. Those blessings will be reflected in an increasingly successful life. So if it's not happening, you are not correctly applying the laws.

> *God not only wants you restored to Him spiritually, He wants you to be healed physically. . . . He wants your light to shine.*

START WITH FAITH

The most basic and fundamental element required for change in our lives is faith. Jesus said, **All things are possible to him that believeth** (Mark 9:23). Interestingly, He didn't say, "All things are *certain* to him that believeth," did He? Or, "All things are definitely going to *work out* if you believe." He said, "All things are possible."

What that tells me is that things will be impossible if we *don't* believe. You see, there is another element involved. It also begins with faith. By faith, you have to believe in your call. You have to believe you are equipped. You have to believe God has given you everything you need to accomplish what He has given you to do.

It does not matter how inadequate you feel or how inappropriate your background may seem. None of those things matter. You have to believe in your call, in your equipping and in the validity of the vocation God has called you to. You have to receive it all by faith.

THE BEGINNING POINT

Your faith is where the power source really is. You cannot doubt your call. You cannot wonder if this is really God. If you are continually wondering if you are supposed to be doing what you're doing, it will only produce a lot of heartache. Stop wasting your time and God's. Go out and get a different job. But if you know that you are called to what you are doing, you have to believe that you are equipped. By faith you must trust that God has empowered you to take the entire city, if that is His plan. You have what it takes to do that.

Now, that is not a commentary on how cool you are. We all know how flawed each of us is. It is a commentary on God's faithfulness to perform what He said He would perform. But He cannot do it if you do not believe it.

So the first thing you have to do is believe in the call on your life. But that is just the beginning.

THE ACTION STEP

Here is where we add what James shows us: **Even so faith, if it hath not works, is dead, being alone** (James 2:17). You can believe until you are blue in the face, but if your behavior does not reflect your heart of faith, then that faith will die unborn on the inside of you.

Paul says something we can all say a hearty amen to: **I delight in the law of God after the inward man** (Rom. 7:22). The law of God, of course, is His Word—not only the written Word of the Scriptures but also the revealed word He has spoken to your heart.

The law of God is also referred to as spiritual seed that is sown and, if properly cultivated, produces a harvest. (Mark 4.) But it is sown in the inward man, in the heart. That is where the seed of God's Word is sown to produce fruit.

In Romans 7:23 Paul continues, **I see another law in my members, warring against the law of my mind, and bringing me into captivity to the law of sin which is in my members.** So there is another law at work in our carnal being. It's called the law of sin and death. The law of sin works through our unregenerated nature and the flesh, the members Paul refers to, and it is in opposition to the law of God that operates from the inward man, where the Word is sown.

The deciding factor is something called "the law of the mind." Understanding and applying the law of the mind determines whether the law of God from your inward man is going to have preeminence in your life or if the law of sin will operate through your members.

Now, these two laws relate to behavior. The mind is between the inward man, which is where the law of God operates, and the members of the flesh, which is where the law of sin operates. When your behavior conforms to the things you believe in your heart, then your faith comes alive.

THE TONGUE-TWISTER TRAP

The apostle Paul himself felt caught between the law of sin and the law of God: **For that which I do I allow not: for what I would, that do I not; but what I hate, that do I** (Rom. 7:15). That is a tongue twister, but he is saying, "I know better than to do a lot of the things I do, but I do them anyway."

He continues in verse 19, **For the good that I would I do not: but the evil which I would not, that I do.** He is not necessarily talking about some great evil, like murder or adultery. It could be a matter of insufficient personal devotional time in the morning. It could be a matter of avoiding gossip at work. He knows what he has to do, but oftentimes he doesn't do it. Why? He loses out to the law of sin working through his members.

Many people think behavior demonstrates what a person really believes in his heart. I have heard preachers say, "Well, you can always tell what people really believe because they are going to do what they believe." That is not always true. If it were, James would not have wasted space in the Bible pointing out the fact that our faith is dead without corresponding action. If behavior automatically followed heart belief, it would not have been necessary to say that. But it doesn't.

We do many things counter to our beliefs for a lot of reasons. For example, we are often reluctant to share our faith because we might be persecuted or rejected. Rejection is a painful thing for the human spirit, so to avoid it, we may shy away from telling someone about Jesus.

Fear of persecution, fear of rejection, fear of bodily harm or fear of financial consequences are all reasons we do not behave in a way that allows our faith to work for us.

So behavior is critical, and the controlling factor is not what you believe. The controlling factor is not what you have disciplined your flesh to do. The controlling factor is something Paul calls, "the law of the mind." Now let's see what the Word of God has to say about it.

12

THE LAW OF THE MIND

What is the law of the mind? Basically this: behavior is a product of imagination. The mind produces a mental image which describes your understanding of reality and your place in it. But it does so on the building blocks of mental imagery. That is the way humans think—in pictures, not in words.

If I said the words "yellow dog," your mind does not see the letters Y-E-L-L-O-W D-O-G. You may see a yellow Labrador retriever. You might see a blonde cocker spaniel. In any event, on the screen of your mind you would see the image of a yellow dog.

That's the imagination at work. You have the capacity to use mental images to build a picture of your life. That picture is created by your imagination, and it is that imagination which ultimately produces behavior.

Imagination is the root of all consistent behavior. All of us have some behaviors which are reactive or spontaneous, based on emotional responses to certain stimuli. But all consistent, patterned behavior is rooted in the imagination. And that consistent behavior, fueled by your imagination, is what gives both direction and movement to your life.

The prophet Habakkuk understood the power of imagination when he proclaimed, **Write the vision, and make it plain upon tables** [tablets] (Hab. 2:2). He was talking about the capacity of the human mind to envision the future. Why is that important? The verse continues, **that he may run that readeth it.** In other words, if the imagination has produced an accurate vision of the future, it will also produce momentum and give impetus to the vision.

THE TOWER OF BABEL

This same concept of imagination appears in Genesis 11:1,4. After the Flood, God told Noah to repopulate the earth. The sons of Noah gave rise to the nations of the earth, **And the whole earth was of one language, and of one speech.... And they said, Go to, let us build us a city and a tower.** Thus the idea for the Tower of Babel was conceived.

Verse 6 continues,

> **And the Lord said, Behold, the people is one, and they have all one language; and this they begin to do: and now nothing will be restrained from them, which they have imagined to do.**

God created the human mind to produce mental imagery; doing follows imagining. But in their imagining, verse 6 adds, **Now nothing will be restrained from them, which they have imagined to do.** Not only is the imagination the root of consistent behavior, but it carries with it a supernatural ability to achieve the imagined objective.

Now, were they some kind of superhuman race? No. Spiritually, they had less than we have. They were not born again. They were not temples of the Holy Spirit with the fullness of God living in them. And yet nothing that they imagined to do, according to God, would be restrained from them. Why? Because that is the way God created the mind. Paul referred to it as the law of the mind. (Rom. 7:23.) And if we can learn to use it properly, it will produce not only direction but irresistible impetus in that direction. That is what the Word says.

Even if the direction is wrong or inconsistent with the will of God, the power of the imagination will produce behavior that will carry a supernatural impetus with it to achieve the imagined objective.

Look at Psalm 2:1: **Why do the heathen rage, and the people imagine a vain thing?** Here the psalmist writes about wrong behavior and something called *vain* imagination. So it would be appropriate to conclude that wrong behavior follows a wrong use of the imagination; vain imaginations cause the heathen to rage. That is what the word *vain* means: "empty, worthless and to no purpose."[1] If you use the capacity of the human mind to build imaginations that are not founded in the Word of God, it will produce wrong behavior.

MEDITATION

Take a look at Psalm 1:2: **But his delight is in the law of the Lord; and in his law doth he meditate day and night.** The word *meditate* is the same Hebrew word translated *imagine* in Psalm 2:1. That is what meditation is—imagining.

We have weird ideas about meditation. We say, "Well, if I want to get healed, I have to sit in the corner and meditate on that word *healing*: healing, healing, healing." No.

As I mentioned, the words *meditate* and *imagine* are rooted in the same Hebrew word, and your concordance will indicate that both words mean "to ponder, to study, to mutter or talk about."[3] Through the psalmist, God is instructing you to build a picture in your mind based on what He has spoken to you in His Word and to your heart. Then allow your imagination to focus on that picture in a continuous sense.

Don't just do it momentarily, but spend time focusing on the picture God's Word has built in your mind.

We could phrase Psalm 1:2 this way: But his delight is in the law of the Lord; and in [God's] law doth he [imagine] day and night.

Now, the reference to meditating day and night should not be a source of frustration. God is simply making a commentary on the fact that your mind never shuts down, even while you sleep. So as best as you know how, make sure the mental imagery produced by your mind is consistent with the truth of God's Word. Don't be casual about it either. Be deliberate.

Are you worried about a wrong someone has done to you? Are you focused on the offense and the hurt and strife it has caused? Is that where you are focusing your attention and pondering and imagining continuously? Then you have come to your "Ai" because that is where the momentum of your efforts will die.

If you will meditate on the law day and night, whatsoever you do shall prosper. (Ps. 1:3.) That's behavior modification. Whatsoever you do will prosper and be blessed when your imagination is shaped by the Word of God, the written Word or the word spoken to your heart. That is God's promise to you.

BUILDING AN IMAGE

The biggest challenge in leadership isn't knowing all the ins and outs of skilled administration. It isn't in being the most dynamic leader in town. God does not say His law works only for those with a college degree or a charismatic personality. The focus is on God's Word, not on the man; therefore, the law of the mind works for anybody.

If you have meditated on the call of God on your life, it occupies your thoughts day and night, and you are feeding the vision with the promises of God's Word, then you will not have to worry about how to behave when your divine opportunity to lead presents itself. God says your behavior will carry you to that opportunity, that prosperity and blessing.

I am not suggesting that you ignore learning the right ways to administrate. Those are skills you should develop. But simply learning those skills is not what will make you a leader. Your focus is the Lord, not necessarily learning all the skills of a corporate manager. Your steps, the Bible says, will be ordered by the Lord. (Ps. 37:23.) If you have allowed your mind to be conformed to the things He has spoken in His Word and by the Holy Spirit, your behavior will automatically be right.

Let your mind function as it was created to function. Let the law of the mind work for you. Build an inner image of what God has called you to do. See it, rather than the problems of the moment. Do not focus on all the injuries and hurts of the past, because if you do, you are squandering the supernatural impetus to achieve the objective God has given you.

You hear people say all the time, "Well, I believe I'm healed, but how do I act that way when I'm still sneezing and coughing?" Or, "I believe God has met my needs, but it hasn't manifested yet. How do I act rich if I'm really not rich yet?"

Saint of God, this is a simple matter. Believing is first. It is not enough to only *imagine*. Faith is your power source. God does not want you to lie about your circumstances. What He instructs you to do is declare the truth of His Word in the face of your circumstances. As you begin to order your behavior in a way that is consistent with the Word in your heart, you will see the desired result.

SHAPED BY CHALLENGES

Most people do not allow their imaginations to be shaped in this manner. Most people allow their imaginations to be shaped by the challenge of the moment or by what they have experienced in the past.

And the more you ponder these facts, the more certain it is that nothing will change. In Philippians 3:13, God, through Paul, basically said, "Hey, man, you have to forget what's in the past." That means put it out of your mind. Otherwise, you will continue to imagine your future on the basis of past experience. You cannot allow your mind to settle on past events, no matter how deep the hurts may be. Everyone has been hurt. Everyone. If you are in the ministry, you have taken some shots. If you are a lay person, you are a target for the enemy. That is a simple fact of life.

Well, what do you do with that?

I do not want to trivialize your situation or minimize the pain you may have felt. But God's Word does not say, "Go find someone who teaches inner healing and spend two years dealing with that." No. He says, "Forget it." Stop feeling sorry for yourself and how bad it is. Get your mind off of it. Forget it! Get back to what God has called you to do.

What has He called you to do? What did He call you to do five years ago? Ten years ago? At the time it was an exciting vision. A big vision. Otherwise you would not have taken the steps you did to see it come to pass. Well, the call hasn't changed. Go back to what God has called you to do. Begin meditating on that.

13

NINETY-ONE ACRES OF VISION

Not too long ago, the church I pastor purchased ninety-one acres of land. We have big plans for that land, but I have to be honest with you—I don't have the foggiest idea how God is going to finance the development of it. But I can rejoice in one certainty: it's not my problem. Praise God! I do not have to figure out how to behave for the next ten years to make it all happen—how to conduct myself before the city council or how to wheel and deal the bankers. I don't have to worry about any of that.

"Well, why not, Mac?" you may ask. Because I can see it. I can see the sanctuary we're going to build there. I can see the orphanage. I can see the family life center. I can see the Bible school. Not with my natural eyes, of course, but in my spirit. I can see all these things in the vision God has birthed in my spirit. And as long as I stay focused on the vision God has given me, my behavior is going to be orchestrated supernaturally by the Holy Spirit to take the ministry in that direction. The same principle is true for you.

Of course, there are going to be a lot of opportunities to get side-tracked by a big challenge. It might be a lawsuit, or perhaps we will encounter some resistance in one corner of the congregation because someone does not agree with what we are doing. Opinions are bound to clash. But I have a choice to make. I can spend my time wondering what they are saying or what they are doing. I can become fearful they might go too far and split the church. Or I can provide the godly leadership I believe we, as a church, need in order to bring us through this project, trusting God for the best outcome. Either way I will have what I focus my attention on. So I must decide what I will allow to consume my imagination.

The law of the mind says that consistent behavior is a product of the imagination. But even more than that, the imagination itself carries with it the supernatural impetus to achieve the imagined objective. So you cannot afford the luxury of dwelling on hurts, past failures or things that should have been. You have to be absolutely determined—utterly, unswervingly determined—to keep your mind filled with what God has called you to do.

It isn't arrogant for me, as a pastor, to think in terms of a 50,000-seat sanctuary. If I can believe it in my heart, imagine it with my mind, and it is consistent with God's call on my life, then, just as God said about Noah's descendants in Genesis 11, there is nothing that will restrain me from what I have imagined to do.

USING YOUR MIND

All of us should be spending more time thinking about the things God has called us to do. In our meditation time we should be developing the glorious ministries in each of our hearts. We should be focused on the coming revival, the healings and the outpouring of God's Spirit, asking Him continually to reveal our part in it.

Use your mind the way God created it to be used. See what He sees. Then there will be more than enough supernatural impetus, energy and ability to carry you there. Do not let brushfires sidetrack you. See things the way God sees them.

OVERCOMING STRONGHOLDS

Here is one of the most vital keys that I know to victory in your life. It involves something the Word calls strongholds. A stronghold is a vain imagination that has been rooted in a person's mind for so long that it has begun to produce obsessive or compulsive behavior.

We usually come to think of obsessive or compulsive behavior as being reserved for the mentally ill. Certainly, we as believers would not want to be thought of in that way. But I have seen many examples in my own behavior which qualify as strongholds. Being too quick to speak and doing so out of anger was one of them. I am pleased to report I have long since had the victory over that. But for a while it was a real problem for me. That stronghold held me back from being able to effectively imagine God's plans for my life.

The way you handle money or view your finances can produce behavior that is not in the best interest of your calling or family life. And it can all be traced back to what the Bible calls strongholds—imaginations that have been in place so long they produce inappropriate behavior. But you can overcome those strongholds and begin seeing your ministry the way God sees it.

You may have some strongholds which keep you from believing for God's best.

BARRIERS TO PROSPERITY AND HEALING

Ironically, the people who respond most readily to the prosperity message are the ones who need it the least. They are the people who already have money. Teaching on prosperity just brings them more blessings. Why? Because they see it. They see it easily because they have lived it.

The people who are usually the hardest to reach, in terms of experiencing financial blessing, are the ones who are born into poverty. Because they have lived in poverty, they really cannot see God's riches being provided for them, at least not as easily as the other person.

God's riches are available to every born-again believer, and, because of the law of the mind, we are all capable of "seeing" them. However, the challenge for those experiencing financial hardship is a lot greater. They have seen God's provision through the eyes of poverty for years, and their imagination is so shaped and so solid that it is difficult for them to escape their way of thinking. That's a stronghold, a vain imagination that has become firmly locked in place.

Similarly, the people who have the most difficulty receiving their healings are those who have been afflicted for a long time. Someone who has been in a wheelchair for twenty years, was born blind, or has had a defect or chronic illness may have developed an understanding of reality which is counter to the Word of God. That person's perception may have become a real stronghold.

That is where strongholds exist—in our perceptions and our imaginations. In 2 Corinthians 10:4-5, Paul instructs us to pull down strongholds and cast down imaginations. Those strongholds occur in the mind, a place where the imagination has focused for so long that the person cannot really see things as God sees them. And that is one of the reasons the anointing has been given to us—to destroy the yoke and set the captives free. Captives to what? Captives to strongholds.

HEARING THE VOICE OF GOD

If you cannot hear the voice of God, He cannot use you as a leader. You have to have His mind, His vision, His purpose and His goal for *your* life before you can effectively direct anyone else's.

When we say a leader must have direction or purpose for the group he is supposed to lead, that seems ridiculously simple and self-evident. But the sad fact is that there are more groups of people, families, organizations, ministries and businesses floundering for lack of direction than there are ones with goals and objectives and a strong sense of direction. When I counsel people, I see a lot more evidence of a lack of direction than I do of good, solid direction.

One of the reasons people do not get promoted in the body of Christ is because they have no sense of purpose. How can God give them responsibility for directing others if they have no direction in their own lives. I'm talking about specific direction here, not generalities.

> *One of the reasons people do not get promoted in the body of Christ is because they have no sense of purpose.*

You can be a man or woman of faith and power because faith *is* power. But without direction your faith will do nothing for you. You can take any power source you can think of, and if you cannot direct that power in a constructive fashion, it will not accomplish anything.

You must have a blueprint that your faith can put substance to. Your blueprint is the vision. Your vision provides the direction God wants you to have in your life. If there is no vision providing direction, you can stay in the Word twenty-four hours a day, you can be a person of faith and still get nowhere in the Kingdom of God. Unless you have God's specific plan for your life, you will be of very little use or service to the Lord. Vision and direction always precede authority and responsibility.

"Is That You, God?"

Many times I hear people say, "If I only knew what the Lord really wanted in this situation, I'd go after it. I wish I knew what God wanted for me in my life."

Why don't many Christians know what God wants for them? The reason is that they are having trouble hearing the voice of God and knowing when He has spoken.

A lot of us think hearing God's voice means having an experience like Moses had. There has to be a burning bush and a voice telling us to take off our shoes; then we will know we are in the presence of God.

Some look for dreams and visions, others for angelic messengers. We're all looking for some supernatural means of hearing what God has for our lives. We would all like it to be that simple when we are confronted with a tough decision. Wouldn't it be nice to have archangel Michael appear and say, "Thus saith the Lord, do this or do that"?

Yet there are so many other ways God speaks to us, if we will just open our hearts and listen to Him.

How do we know when He is talking to us? How can we be sure we can run with what we have heard and not waver back and forth, wondering if we are in His will or not?

A lot of us just let life happen to us. Sometimes we are that way unconsciously. We don't really think we can make it big. We did not come from a strong family background, or we are not prominent socially. We are just kind of average, and we have no reason to expect too much more. So we simply let life happen.

Sometimes, even after we have heard the Word and begun to exercise our faith, we still live from one day to the next. Life happens to us, and depending on whether we like what happens or not, we blame it on God or the Devil. But God wants every one of our steps to be ordered. He wants us to be certain of where we are going. He is not the author of confusion. And He has made a way for us to know His direction for our lives.

ESTABLISHING EVERY WORD

This is the third time I am coming to you. In the mouth of two or three witnesses shall every word be established.

2 Corinthians 13:1

When God speaks to you or me—when He speaks to anyone—He will do so in at least two different ways. That does not necessarily mean He will give you two or three Scriptures for everything.

We are three-part beings, right? We are a spirit being, we have a soul and we live in a body. God is not going to ignore any of those areas of your life when He communicates with you. He is going to minister His will and His direction to you in each of those areas.

So not only in the realm of the spirit, but in the soul realm and the physical realm, you will hear God speaking to you about the direction your life is to take. One will confirm the other, the other will confirm the other and so forth, until there are so many confirmations that you will look back and feel ridiculous because you did not hear what God was saying long before.

That's the way you can find your "ninety-one acres of vision"— God's specific direction for *your* life.

14

DIRECTION AND GUIDANCE

And the very God of peace sanctify you wholly; and I pray God your whole spirit and soul and body be preserved blameless unto the coming of our Lord Jesus Christ.

1 Thessalonians 5:23

What does the phrase *sanctify you wholly* mean? It means to separate you completely unto God. God is concerned that all three of your life's areas—the spirit, the soul and the body—be separated unto Him. He is going to give you two or three witnesses and ample direction in each of these parts of your being in order to guide and direct your life.

How does God communicate direction to your spirit man? The primary and most basic way is through His Word.

All scripture is given by inspiration of God, and is profitable for doctrine, for reproof, for correction, for instruction in righteousness: that the man of God may be perfect, thoroughly furnished unto all good works.

2 Timothy 3:16,17

This is our standard of evaluation. The Bible is a book of principles: You are not supposed to kill. You are not supposed to commit adultery. You are not supposed to lie. You are not supposed to backbite and gossip. It gives you standards, principles you are to abide by, which will give general direction to your life. However, it does not always deal with the specifics.

For example, you may have two or three decisions to make—whether to buy this house or that house, take this job or that job, marry this person or that person and so forth. Houses, jobs and spouses are all fine with God—having them agrees with His Word—but you need specific direction.

> **For as many as are led by the Spirit of God, they are the sons of God. For ye have not received the spirit of bondage again to fear; but ye have received the Spirit of adoption, whereby we cry, Abba, Father. The Spirit itself beareth witness with our spirit, that we are the children of God.**
>
> **Romans 8:14-16**

This is what we refer to as "the inward witness," and this is how you receive more specific direction for your life.

It is like that settled feeling you get when you turn to your best friend and ask, "Do you agree with this?" and he or she says, "Yes, most definitely."

When you sense an inward witness, you come into agreement with the Spirit who lives inside you. You feel settled and comfortable because **the Spirit itself beareth witness with our spirit.**

There are other ways God speaks to us in the soulish realm and the physical realm to help clarify the times we are not really sure we have received an inward witness.

But let me say this: the Holy Spirit is a gentleman. He does not push. He does not pressure. If you feel pressured or pushed, it isn't

God. The Bible says haste is sin. If you are feeling pushed into a situation because it just won't wait—the deal is so good, the job is just perfect, a man like that doesn't come around twice—just say, "See you later." Because God does not push, and He does not pressure.

The Holy Spirit will give you a sense of peace and knowing and quiet confidence. If you do not have peace about a situation, don't move on it. Wait until you are sure the direction you receive does bring an inner witness and a lasting peace, and then take action. The Word of God is your measuring stick, and it gives you general direction; the inward witness gives you specific direction.

We have said that as three-part beings we have a soul. Our soul consists of our mind, our will and our emotions, and it is our will that is the decision-maker. The weighing, measuring, evaluating part of the soul is our mind, or our intellect.

God gave you your mind to use. That may sound like a foolish thing to say, but a lot of us turn our minds off when we are born again, because we hear so much about the carnal mind. God never said the mind was bad; He said it was bad for your mind to be ruled by the flesh. You have to use your mind.

God gave us our ability to reason, to weigh, to measure and to evaluate. God gave us common sense. He does not expect us to float around on a little faith cloud and never use our minds. In fact, in Isaiah 1:18, God said, **Come now, and let us reason together.**

USING THE MIND OF CHRIST

Part of the miraculous transformation of being born again is that we receive the mind of Christ. Why? So we can let it lie dormant? No. So we can use it as God wants us to use it, in accordance with His Word.

Do ye not know that the saints shall judge the world? and if the world shall be judged by you, are ye unworthy to judge the smallest matters? Know ye not that we shall

judge angels? how much more things that pertain to this life?

1 Corinthians 6:2,3

God said that you are to judge the things which pertain to this life. How do you do that? You use your experience, your intellect and your reason to weigh, measure, evaluate and make judgments of the things of this life. If you lack the wisdom to make an evaluation, ask for it, and He will give you as much wisdom as you need to make the right decision. (James 1:5.) That is one of the ways God speaks to you.

Perhaps you are considering a new job, an opportunity you feel pretty good about in your spirit and which offers nothing contrary to the Word, but that doesn't make the figures work. It's just not going to produce enough income for you and your family.

I would suggest that God is speaking to you through your reasoning ability. It does not make sense to take a job you cannot live on. So unless that good feeling in your spirit is a solid knowing that God wants you in this job, pass. Believe Him for a job that will pay better.

Sometimes we spiritualize things so much that we ignore the good common sense God gave us. We have become too spiritual to pay attention to the gray matter between our ears. But that is why God put it there, and that is one of the ways He will speak to you, through your own natural reason. When God is speaking to you to do something, it will make good sense from more than one viewpoint for you to do it.

THE PHYSICAL DIMENSION

We are a spirit, we have a soul and we live in a physical realm. We deal with physical circumstances and situations and relationships and people.

For every one that useth milk [or has no experience] **is unskilful in the word of righteousness: for he is a babe. But strong meat belongeth to them that are of full age, even**

those who by reason of [habitual] **use have their senses exercised to discern both good and evil.**

Hebrews 5:13,14

Your physical senses can be trained to discern between good and evil. You do not have to close your eyes, float away and try to forget what your spirit is saying. When you reach a certain point in the Lord, your physical senses can discern between good and evil because you have trained them to do so.

God directs us in the physical realm by what theologians call "providential circumstance." In more normal English, we call it "open doors."

> *God directs us in the physical realm by what theologians call "providential circumstance." In more normal English, we call it "open doors."*

Satan opens and closes doors, too, because he is the prince of this world. He opened a door to Adam, who handed his God-given dominion over to the Devil. You must be aware that God is not the only one who opens and closes doors.

But here is what I want you to understand about doors: God will not give you specific direction for your life and then keep the door shut. If you reach a certain point and that door is shut and will not open, either God has not called you there, or if He has, it isn't time yet. It's one of the two.

Many of us spend a great deal of time trying in the name of faith to kick down doors God does not want opened. When He tells you to do something, and you get to that point, then if it's God, the door will open.

You say, "Well, if the Devil opens doors, how do I know I'm going through the right one?" Rely on your soul: your reason, your common sense and your judgment. And rely on your spirit: your inward witness, your unshakable peace and the circumstances' compatibility with the Word of God. If everything checks out, the open door is of God, and you should step through it.

OPEN DOORS

When we were looking for a new building, the first location we were really serious about was on a road near our present location. In the natural, this option appeared to be consistent with the Word of God. It bore witness with my spirit. (The truth was, I wanted out of our old building so badly I could taste it.) And it appeared we could make it work financially. But I couldn't get the door to open.

Every time we sat down with the owners to negotiate, another problem would come up. The city council got involved, and it looked like a solid dead end. Then all of a sudden, God finally got my attention: "That's not where I want you."

I immediately stopped pushing to acquire that space, and it was less than two weeks later that our current building became available. Just like that, every detail came together. The doors were open where He had called us to be.

That is a sure indicator of whether or not you are on track with God.

I know some folks who had a genuine call of God on their lives. They knew they were called to the ministry, but the doors were not open to them. Common sense and reason said it should have been happening. Even their good judgment told them they had heard from God.

God did call them into the ministry, but closed doors were an indicator to them that His due season had not arrived.

God has a time and a season for everything. And it is important that you don't miss His timing. Wait on Him. Stay in faith. He will reveal His timetable.

Christians have a way of getting ahead of God. I know I have. We get impatient. We cannot wait to get out there and do what He has put in our hearts to do. But we have to understand that this is one of the main ways—providential circumstances, or open doors—He will indicate that His timing has arrived.

God directs us through His Word and specifically through His inner witness, but He also guides us through open doors.

15

SHAPING YOUR VISION

As leaders we must focus on three areas: vision, communication and motivation. Vision is what gives general direction to everything you do in your life. It keeps you on the right path. It keeps you from veering to the right or to the left.

Vision is what orients the activity in your life in a particular direction. There are several kinds of vision we must have. We must also impart them to those who are working for us if we are going to be successful leaders.

THE BIG PICTURE CORPORATELY

When you think of vision, does something like this come to your mind? "Our vision is to win 35,000 people to the Lord this year!" Or, "We're going to generate $7 million of income!"

That is not vision. Those are short-term objectives.

Vision is your mental understanding, your mental perception of reality. Vision is how you see life and how you see yourself fitting into it.

Vision encompasses a wide range of understanding. This is the part we could call "The Big Picture." Everyone has to have an understanding of the big picture. The guy working in the mail room has to understand how his daily effort fits into the big picture—not just his eight-hour work day, but God's plan for his life, for this nation and for the world.

Every one of us has an eternal calling that transcends all dispensational lines. What I mean by that is, every one of us has a calling that is applicable to the age in which we live. Every one of us has an individual calling that is shaped by the gifts and talents and abilities unique to us. All of these things add together to provide the kind of vision that gives meaningful direction to our lives and our ministries.

You have all seen those picture puzzles with thousands of pieces. When you scatter those pieces on a rug, it is impossible to make sense of them. If you did not have the picture on the top of the box to show you what the big picture looked like, putting it together would be nearly hopeless.

Life is that way. There are thousands of things which affect the quality of our lives and our success in life. Those things are scattered all across the canvas of our day. If we did not have a big picture to show us where to fit each piece, life would be a lot harder than it already is. We have to have the big picture. It keeps us properly oriented.

BACK TO BASICS

What does God say is your eternal calling and purpose? All of us have the same eternal calling and purpose. There is only one eternal calling which can transcend all dispensational lines, individual gifts, talents and abilities, and that is to rule and reign with Jesus Christ for all eternity.

Rule and reign over what? Two or three square feet of terra firma? No. Over a universe populated with untold billions of galaxies containing billions of suns which contain billions of planetary bodies. And I will assure you there is other life there, not just because the odds almost make it a certainty mathematically but because God says so in His Word. He talks about winged creatures and four-headed beasts, not to mention the angelic host.

So we know there is a universe so broad and so wide that we cannot even conceive of the boundaries intellectually. And He said that one of the main reasons He created you is so you can rule and reign (or manage and administrate) the vastness of this creation with all of its life forms on His behalf.

That is what we are here to learn. If you cannot learn how to influence a few people in your neighborhood, if you cannot learn how to lead in an environment as limited as it is now, how will you ever handle what comes later?

God put us on this earth to learn these lessons so we don't do any damage on a cosmic scale. Then when we have learned these lessons, we graduate to our eternal calling.

That's what the parable of the talents in Matthew 25 is all about. A lord goes on a journey to a far country and entrusts his estate and all of his belongings to three servants, each **according to his several ability,** verse 15 says.

DISTRIBUTION AND REWARD

The master's resources were not distributed equally to the three servants: one had five talents, another had two and another had one, each according to his own ability. It does not matter how much God gives you to manage. We sometimes look at the people who are given huge amounts of authority and think, "Wow, their reward is going to be great!" But you will notice that the ones who had the five talents and the two talents received the same reward. It has to do with making the best of what God gives you, regardless of how much that is.

So the lord went on a journey to a far country, and when he returned, he took an account of what he had entrusted to his servants. The two servants who received a "well done" were the ones who had brought increase to their lord's kingdom. This story, saint of God, is a parable about God's Kingdom.

God expects you to bring an increase—not for you personally—but to the Kingdom of God. And what is the principle that governs increase in the Kingdom? The principle of sowing and reaping.

Increase in the Kingdom is not based on how much you save in the bank or invest in stocks. You bring increase to the Kingdom of God through the principle of sowing and reaping. That is why Jesus said in Mark 4:13 that if you do not understand the parable of the sower, you are not going to understand any of the other parables. He said the whole Kingdom of God works on this principle to produce increase: sowing and reaping.

How you use the resources He has entrusted to you—some of which may be human, some of which may be material or financial—will determine whether or not you will hear what Matthew 25:21 says: **Well done, thou good and faithful servant: thou hast been faithful over a few things, I will make thee ruler over many things: enter thou into the joy of thy lord.** The bottom line has to be, did you use your resources in such a way as to produce an increase in the Kingdom of God? You see, our eternal rulership is going to depend on how well we learn the very lessons we are learning today.

PUTTING THINGS IN PERSPECTIVE

The purpose of influencing people and attaining a vision of what God has called you to do is to bring increase to the Kingdom of God. It is not to make you rich. It is not to position you to retire early so you can play golf for the last twenty years of your life. God does not want you to work till you're sixty-five years old at the same job, retire with a gold watch and die without ever having brought increase to the Kingdom.

We are talking about eternity now. We are talking about what is really important. We get our eyes on this life and say, "This is the big deal, right here. This is it in a nutshell." No. We must get away from that view. James said, **For what is your life? It is even a vapour, that appeareth for a little time, and then vanisheth away** (James 4:14). You are being prepared for eternity. How many of you would like to rule three or four galaxies? You *should* want that.

> *When you add God's plan for your life to the vision He imparts to other believers, God's redemptive plan for mankind is promoted.*

How is God's vision for your life going to produce increase in the Kingdom? If you are not running your own ministry or your own business, you have to view your contribution in terms of the organization you are a part of right now. How can you best help them to fulfill *their* vision? Your means of bringing increase to the Kingdom is through assisting their efforts, which is going to produce an increase for the Kingdom of God.

If you do have your own ministry or business, you have to make it clear to those who work for you that the part they play is important because they bring increase to what God has called you to do. Their efforts will help you fulfill *your* heavenly vision, but it will affect *their* eternity.

When you add God's plan for your life to the vision He imparts to other believers, God's redemptive plan for mankind is promoted. Then, as far as I am concerned, this deal can end. Let's all get our "Well done" from the Master and go on to rule and reign with Jesus.

Rulership means to administer on behalf of someone else. It implies delegated authority, because He is the Lord. But we will rule and reign *with* Him for an eternity. *Selah*; stop and think about that for a moment.

EXPANDING YOUR PERSPECTIVE

It is an awesome thing to think the Creator of the universe wants our help in administrating the vastness of this creation, is it not? That viewpoint can sometimes strike the wrong religious chord—the idea that God wants our help to do anything. He is all-knowing, ever-present and all-powerful. He couldn't possibly need our help.

Yes, He does! We fit into His plan of universal administration over an eternity. That is why He made us. We are the only creation made in His image and likeness. We have been given dominion and authority over all the earth. We are the only creatures able to practice leadership principles in this life, principles which are going to make us effective administrators for Him in eternity.

This is the training ground. We are to use our anointings, our gifts and our callings of God to multiply the Kingdom. Your eternal calling to administrate on the Lord's behalf is going to be determined by your faithfulness to steward your leadership abilities here.

I used to think that over the period of years before Jesus returns there would be a few billion believers. All of us have been told we will rule and reign with Him. Well, if my math is correct, that means I would be fortunate to get two or three square feet of terra firma to rule and reign over.

Then through more study of the Scriptures, I realized that the Bible talks about the emissaries on this earth after the Millennium. When Jesus returns, there are going to be many people who do not know He has returned. So there are still going to be emissaries on this earth. But those emissaries the Bible talks about are the Jewish people.

So what does that leave for the Gentiles?

A UNIVERSE TO RULE

Well, it leaves Gentiles to rule a universe so vast that technology has not yet found its edge. The more powerful our telescopes are and the more solar systems and star systems we find, the more billions and billions of suns and planets we discover. The numbers are incredible. The challenges which confront us here are intended to accomplish one thing: to make us more effective administrators on a universal, eternal scale. Our minds need to be renewed to this truth.

Let me give you an example. For centuries the world has programmed women to think that a woman's place is only in the home, raising the children and administrating her household. Therefore, what woman can actually see herself ruling and reigning in eternity? But that is the truth of God's Word.

God says He needs us. He needs us in His eternal scheme of things. And the lessons we learn here in this life—about love and faith and sowing and reaping and gentleness and kindness and goodness and patience and consistency and diligence—are the lessons designed to train us for an eternity to come.

You are not just struggling along here for sixty to seventy years and then retiring to heaven to lay in a hammock and sip juice for an eon or two. This is serious business. We are learning the lessons that are going to determine the extent of our eternal rulership as we administrate for an eternity on behalf of our Lord.

It's all about leadership. It's all about administrating, organizing and promoting the Kingdom, the plan and the purpose of God. That is our eternal calling.

Our Dispensational Calling

Our dispensational calling is what keeps things in perspective. Remember, your perception of reality determines how you act. If ruling and reigning on an eternal level is real to you, it will shrink your day-to-day problems down to size, won't it? It will keep them in perspective.

An eternal view can bring our problems down to size. Things which ordinarily control so many people's behavior, like fears and anxieties, just melt away.

For example, fear of death controls many people's behavior without their awareness. They will not go swimming. Why? Fear of death. They will not fly in an airplane. Why? Fear of death. The word cancer strikes fear in their heart. Why? Fear of death.

So much of our behavior is unconsciously controlled by the way we have been mentally programmed; how we act determines what we impart as we relate to other people. That is why it is so important for the truth of God's Word to become reality to us, not just mental assent.

When you allow your mind to create a mental image, it produces behavior. If you have a mental image of the wrong thing, it will produce the wrong behavior. If you are envisioning your life worked out within the parameters of God's Word, it will produce behavior which is correct and in the right direction. That is why Paul emphasizes the need to renew our minds. (Rom. 12:2.)

The world's way of doing things and looking at things has so permeated our thinking that we must make a conscious effort to see our lives within the context and framework of God's Word. His is an eternal calling.

Rulership, leadership, reigning with Jesus, leadership—all these things are so basic to what life is all about. Yet we hardly ever see it that way. So our behavior is modified, but in a negative sense, by what the world has told us.

But when the truth of God's Word becomes our reality, problems come into perspective. Anxieties and fears, which might keep us from acting or reacting as we should, are reduced to choices we make rather than pitfalls we are unable to avoid. God's ways have to become reality, because, as they do, we gain a clearer understanding of our dispensational calling. This narrows our vision, or the way we see life, a little more.

A TWO-PRONGED ATTACK

The two prongs to our dispensational mandate or calling are evangelism and discipleship.

A *dispensation* is the ordering or management of the world by delegated divine authority. Dispensationally, that is, the management principle Jesus made us subject to was the Great Commission in Matthew 28:19-20. Jesus said we have been commissioned to preach the gospel to all the world. How do we do that? Evangelism is the first prong of our dispensational calling. Then He said to go into the highways and the byways and bring them into His house so they could be fed a banquet of God's Word, grow up, mature and become a part of the glorious Church. (Luke 14:23,24.)

Discipleship, the second prong, is preaching the Word to see people saved and grow up spiritually. Everything you do ought to be measured by its effectiveness in achieving one of those two dispensational callings.

If you are going to administrate on an eternal scale for our Lord, if this is reality to you, then it completely restructures your behavior.

Once you realize that everything you do should contribute to one of two things—getting people saved or helping them grow in God's Word—it completely restructures your use of time and your use of money. Your behavior is completely altered. Your behavior changes because you have finally grasped the big picture, which keeps you running on the right track.

The reason ministries and people get sidetracked and sometimes even fall into gross deception is that they lose sight of the big picture. The leadership loses the ability to communicate the goals and purposes effectively with the people who are working to bring them about. Consequently, the workers seldom produce what the leaders desire. Even if the production of tangible goods is maintained, the intangible problems—strife, division, unrest, dissatisfaction—will be present because the leadership is unclear of its objectives.

Your view of the call on your life and how you fit in the plan of God will affect how you behave toward those who work for you and how they respond to your behavior.

This has to be the first focus of a leader's effort—to develop the vision within himself and then to develop it in the lives of those for whom he has been given responsibility.

16

YOUR INDIVIDUAL VISION

The Bible tells us we are the people who have been chosen to rule and reign with Jesus. We are the Church which has been mandated to evangelize and disciple the world. This vision applies to everyone who is a part of the family of God.

There is also the matter of individual vision and destiny and callings which relate to your uniqueness as a human being. No two people have the same combination of gifts, talents, abilities and anointings. Yours are completely unique to you. Therefore, God's calling for you is different from His calling for anyone else. But we have to understand the general truths, the big picture we just talked about, to keep us on track.

What about your individual callings? The Bible does not record whom you should marry, where you should live, whom you should work for, what your vocation should be, whether you should attend college or not and if so, where or what you should study. Those things are not in the Bible, but they are just as crucial to your effective functioning as a leader in the body of Christ. You have to have answers to all of these specifics before you can meaningfully contribute to God's overall purpose and communicate direction to anyone else.

But if the Bible doesn't tell you the answers, where do you go for them?

GETTING YOUR VISION

How are you going to get the vision for your life, and how will you fit into the larger vision of God's plan? Paul answered the same questions for the Corinthian believers: **But as it is written, Eye hath not seen, nor ear heard, neither have entered into the heart of man, the things which God hath prepared for them that love him** (1 Cor. 2:9).

Paul is saying that you cannot even imagine or comprehend, naturally speaking, the things God has prepared for you. He has a marvelous destiny planned just for you. It is so unique that He says no eye has seen it nor ear heard it.

In other words, you are not going to discover this divinely appointed destiny in college or at a business seminar. Your best friend will not be able to advise you on what it might be. Even your parents do not have a clue. Because eye has not seen it and ear has not heard it, you cannot even imagine it. That is how magnificent God's plan for your life is. It is mind-blowing, I know, but we need to have our minds blown.

"Well, Pastor," you say, "if we cannot even conceive of it, how do we discover it?"

Verse 10 says, **But God hath revealed them unto us by his Spirit.** The Holy Spirit's ministry in your life lies primarily in the revelation of God's plan for you. And that is the only way it will come—by revelation of the Holy Spirit. It will not come through any natural channel, through a book, a person or through any institution we as humans have cultivated or developed. It will come through the Holy Spirit.

Now we have received, not the spirit of the world, but the spirit which is of God; that we might know the things [such as our divinely appointed destiny] **that are freely given us of God. Which things also we speak, not in the words which man's wisdom teacheth, but which the Holy Ghost teacheth; comparing spiritual things with spiritual.**

1 Corinthians 2:12,13

Verse 13 in the Amplified Bible says, **And we are setting these truths forth in words not taught by human wisdom but taught by the (Holy) Spirit.** What truths? The truths regarding God's plan for you and His destiny for your life. If you're going to fit meaningfully into God's overall plan, you have to have His vision for your life. His destiny and His plan for you are the truths set forth in words **not taught by human wisdom, but taught by the (Holy) Spirit, combining** *and* **interpreting spiritual truths with spiritual language** [to those who possess the (Holy) Spirit] (v. 13 AMP).

In a nutshell, you receive the plan of God for your life as you yield to the Holy Spirit's ministry: as you pray in tongues, as you sit before Him quietly, allowing Him to pray through you, combining and interpreting spiritual truths with spiritual language. Remember, it is the Holy Spirit's ministry to reveal God's plan to you.

Spending the Time

Many management gurus from some of the largest corporations in the world mandate a period of time each day for their young, up-and-coming executives to engage in creative thinking. The world has learned the value of letting the imagination paint the vision on the canvas of the mind. How I pray the body of Christ would catch the importance of this principle—something the world has been using successfully for many years.

For the Christian who is filled with the Holy Spirit, during your "creative thinking," or meditation, God speaks to your heart about your life. It is when He will show you the things eye has yet to see and ear has yet to hear, and neither has entered the heart of man. It will blow you away.

His plan for your life is great and grand and wonderful. Only within the scope of His plan will you find the greatest measure of contentment, the greatest measure of satisfaction and the greatest measure of success in life. But you have to have the plan first. And that comes only by spending time with the Lord.

If you do not know where you are going, if you do not have sufficient detail for your life, you must spend more time with God. Ask Him to reveal these things to you. Sit quietly before Him, and they will begin to come to you.

If they don't, you are not being quiet enough mentally. It does no good to sit there while your mind is wandering off to a game of golf or a business meeting.

No. We must yield to the ministry of the Holy Spirit, and the primary way we do that is by praying in the Spirit. Paul says in verse 13, **Which things** [the things He has prepared for you] **also we speak, not in the words which man's wisdom teacheth, but which the Holy Ghost teacheth; comparing spiritual things with spiritual.**

It is a very super*natural* process, but it does not require you to be super*spiritual*. It simply requires you to take time to do it, because God wants His plan known to everybody.

So if the vision for your life isn't clear, simply spend more time quietly in the presence of the Lord, yielding to the ministry of the Holy Spirit, and it will become clear. He might not show it to you all at one time. That would probably blow you out of the water! There may seem to be gaps here and there, but be faithful to take what He does give you and believe it. You *will* receive it.

MARY HAD IT RIGHT

Believing what God shows you is as important as believing the written Word of God. We have little trouble looking at the Scriptures and saying, as Mary did, **Be it done unto me according to thy word** (Luke 1:38). But when we are in the prayer closet and He gives us ideas by the Holy Ghost, we may start second-guessing ourselves. We may say, "I don't know if that's really God. That's pretty big. I don't have that much education. I don't know if I have that kind of clout." We begin questioning what is just as important for us to receive by faith as the written Word of God.

> . . . "Be it done unto me, Lord, according to Thy Word. If You say that's for me, then I choose to believe it."

When the Holy Spirit begins to reveal God's plan, say, "Be it done unto me, Lord, according to Thy Word. If You say that's for me, then I choose to believe it." You might say, "How do I know that was from God? It could have been my flesh. Maybe I just thought it up. Maybe it was the Devil!"

Well, there is a really easy test to determine whether or not what you are sensing is from the Lord or from your carnal nature. Those are the only two possibilities. It comes either from your carnal mind, which is at enmity with God (Rom. 8:7), or from the illumination of the Holy Spirit.

GRATIFICATION AND GLORY

How do you know which is which? The way you can always tell if you're sensing God's Spirit or your own carnal nature is by how much self-gratification is involved. If the desire or the idea is intended to benefit principally you, then it is not from the Lord. If, on the other hand, it has a wider impact that reaches out to touch others and change them, taking the gospel to the world, then it is the Lord. It's that simple.

I am not suggesting that God will never lead you in a direction which benefits you personally. Healing falls into that category. But why do you want to be healed? The Bible says, **Ye ask, and receive not, because ye ask amiss, that ye may consume it upon your lusts** (James 4:3). Once you have asked in faith, you still might not receive what you have asked for if your motive is purely self-concern.

If the only reason you want to be healed is to be a comfortable couch potato with no pain, or so you can go out and do a little partying, then you are asking for the wrong motive. God wants you to be healed so you can testify to others of His goodness and His love, influencing them for the cause of Christ.

Why are you asking the Lord to prosper you? Is it so you can retire early and buy what you want? Or is it so you can truly have a greater impact for the Lord, supporting missionaries or feeding the poor?

What are your underlying motives? If you really want to know whether the things that come to you in your quiet time are truly of the Holy Ghost or not, ask yourself, "Who does it primarily benefit? Does it bring glory to me or to God? How will it affect souls?" Be honest with yourself, because God knows your heart.

If the honest answer is, "Lord, this is something I see bringing increase to your Kingdom," then it's of Him.

Don't be casual about it if there are any significant gaps in your understanding of what God has for your life. You will need to spend time with Him in order to fill those gaps. He will show you which way to go. And when He does, do not write it off as a pizza dream. Say, "Be it done unto me according to Thy Word. Lord, I receive it. It's a big vision, but it is Your responsibility to bring it to pass. You showed it to me. I receive it by faith. Now You bring it to me."

A PURPOSE AND A DESTINY

As you pray in the Holy Spirit and open your heart to God, you have to have the understanding that there is a divinely appointed destiny for each one of us. You have to be looking for it.

That is why many Christians, Spirit-filled people, never seem to know where they are going. They do not realize that this is one of the primary ministries of the Holy Spirit—to reveal God's plan to them so their vision is meaningful.

As you pray in the Holy Ghost in your private devotional time, expecting Him to show you things about your life—where you fit into ministry, what your role should be and so forth—ideas will start coming to your mind. A dream will start forming in your heart, a dream that will propel your life and motivate you the way nothing ever has before.

If this were a process all Christians deliberately pursued, there would be a lot fewer of them getting in the wrong place and being disappointed, failing here because they missed God or failing there because nothing came together.

The Holy Spirit is faithful to reveal His plan to you. He will make that dream so real on the inside of you that you can't stand it. It will become etched on your heart in a way that drives you toward your goal. You will have supernatural impetus behind you.

I am saying all this because I have met so many people who loved God and were filled with gifts and talents and abilities. They desired to be a meaningful part of what God is doing in the earth but never seemed to fit, never seemed to succeed, because none of these principles were clear to them.

You have to understand vision; you have to see the big picture. You are being groomed for eternal administration and management of God's creation. Dispensationally, we define our administrative efforts within the framework of evangelism and discipleship, and you have a specific place to fit into that plan.

You are not going to know where you fit, however, unless it is revealed to you by the Holy Spirit. You must spend time on a regular basis, sitting in His presence, praying in the Spirit, letting Him reveal the dream as well as His plan for unfolding it. When you do that, you will be prepared to take steps in the right direction.

17

THE DREAM—YOUR DREAM

The dream God reveals will be different for everyone. Depending on gifts, talents and abilities, your dream may be to have the most dynamic youth ministry the world has ever seen. Or because of your technical orientation, your dream may be to do a media complex that produces television broadcasts that are seen around the world. You have to dream big. Remember, the biggest way we limit God is through our unwillingness to acknowledge His "bigness" in our dreaming.

Listen to your heart. What is your fondest desire? Let the Holy Spirit elaborate on that, and He'll begin showing you what will give you the impetus you'll need to see you through to its realization.

Once the dreaming part has been done, don't stop there. God does not give you a dream without also giving you a plan to realize the dream. But always be sure your dream can be realized within the context of the organization in which God has planted you.

EARLY LESSONS

In the earlier days of our church some people came to me with grand visions. One man had a vision burning on his heart for a mission outreach to Haiti. He was sure it was of God—and I do not deny that—but it did not coincide with our ministry's vision. We were involved in an outreach to Russia at the time. Consequently, his enthusiasm for the vision in his heart caused him to bring division to our church.

He began drawing disciples to his vision, and he could not understand when I went to him and said, "Brother, what you're doing is wrong. It's not that you haven't heard from God or that it isn't a good vision. You're simply in the wrong place. There is a place where you can get connected and your vision can be realized within the framework of that ministry's vision. You'll have to find where that is. Then you won't be divisive. Then your participation won't be controversial or confusing. Then it won't split our effort. Then you can make a meaningful contribution."

You must understand the importance of seeing your dreams and visions realized within the context of the organization that God has opened to your participation. If that is not possible, you must stop your efforts until it is. Why? Because that is a principle of submission and authority. If, after seeking the Lord, you know you are to continue your efforts, then you are in the wrong place. You must move on, or you will potentially become a divisive influence within that organization.

Many people use positions as stepping-stones to set up their own thing. That is wrong; it is unhealthy for you, and it is unhealthy for the organization. However, if you will see the realization of your dream within the context of the mission you are submitted to, it will help keep your heart right. It will keep you from inadvertently seeing your participation as a stepping-stone to something higher and better. You cannot give your all to that organization if you are only using them to get what you want, because if that is your attitude, God won't promote you.

Luke 16:12 says if you are not faithful in that which is another man's, who will entrust you with that which is your own?

AVOIDING CONFLICTS OF INTEREST

God may have shown you that you will have your own enterprise at some point. But if you let that understanding be the motivating force in your life, then you are going to have conflicts of interest. To be faithful in that which is another man's, you must give him 100 percent of your support in the pursuit of his godly vision. Through that experience God will test your character and, specifically, your faithfulness.

If you prove yourself faithful to another person's vision, the day will come when God will entrust you with your own.

Most people will see their God-given vision realized within the context of a larger organization's effort. That is a simple organizational truth, and even God works within that framework. Organization is His idea, by the way; it didn't originate in the secular environment. So it is likely your dream will be realized within the framework of a larger endeavor.

But if you are called to lead your own enterprise and at some point He separates you to lead an effort that could be called your own, you will never be absolved from being faithful to that which is another's. If you ever stop serving other people's efforts and focus entirely on your own, you will wither and die.

I am connected with other ministers whom I consider my fathers in the faith. I am obligated scripturally and by the Spirit to be faithful to help them in the areas my gifts and abilities allow. Actually, there are three or four men to whom God has connected me with in this regard, and when God opens the door of opportunity, I am committed to serving them. If I ever stop doing that, I can forget the ministry He has given me here in Minneapolis, because it will become ingrown, introverted and self-serving.

Serving others will not only open your place of calling, but it will also establish you in it.

A RIGHT VIEW OF MINISTRY

Let me review for a moment the distance we have covered so far. As you have prayed in the Spirit, God has given you a vision. You have continued in prayer to get the big picture. You have measured the validity of the vision by asking a couple of key questions: Are God's purposes advanced because of the vision? Does the vision contribute to the big picture in some fashion?

Once you have measured it against those standards and it is a settled issue in your heart, the vision must fit into the framework of the organization which is opened to your present participation. The purpose of that is to keep your heart right, to ensure you are not using that business as a stepping-stone and because your faithfulness there is what makes it possible for God to promote you.

When a vocation is developed in this manner, following these steps, everyone involved benefits. It's the law of synergy: the combined effect of working together exceeds the sum of the individual gifts, abilities and anointings.

If a church's success were dependent on the gifts in the pastoral staff alone, the ministry's impact would be limited to only those whom the pastors themselves could touch. That is not a negative commentary on the pastoral staff, but it takes all of us to get the job done. No one gift, no one set of talents is going to do it. So as the pastors make room for you to realize your vision—not to do your own thing but to develop within the scope of the church's vision—then add your creativity and your gifts to theirs, and the whole ministry grows exponentially.

ENVIRONMENT FOR MINISTRY

As the pastor of Living Word Christian Center, I am convinced of the necessity to provide an environment in which people can pursue their vision within the context of our ministry. We want to see, for example, drug addicts set free and restored to a useful place in society. That is something that fits within the scope of our vision, but I have absolutely no gifts which equip me to minister to them.

However, God has brought people to our ministry who do. They not only have the desire, they have a clear vision for it. They know exactly the track to run on to get the rehabilitation center going and the transitional-living complex erected. They know what to do because the vision is in them.

Now, if I had said, "Since I don't have the skills to do this, it must not be for this ministry," I would have shut down what God wants to do to expand the influence and impact of that ministry. No. My job as a leader is to make sure the ministries in our church develop within the framework of our vision. Once it falls within the framework of our vision, as a leader it's my responsibility to be a resource to them in fulfilling what is in their hearts. Then both ministries will grow and impact the city in a very influential way.

> *Let them know you want God to work through them to expand the impact of the organization. Then God will use the gifts in each of them . . .*

As a leader you must give the people who work for you that latitude. You cannot limit them to "Come to work at 8 and leave at 5 and do A,B,C,D and E." They may have to do that, but let them know that you are open to the Spirit of God's working through them. They must know you welcome their ideas and suggestions, creative ways of producing greater output or more efficient ways of doing what they need to do. Let them know you want God to work through them to expand the impact of the organization. Then God will use the gifts in each of them to bring growth to their area of service, which in turn will bring growth to the overall enterprise.

As people with leadership responsibilities pursue the vision in their hearts in that manner and give the people beneath them the opportunity to pursue the vision in their hearts in that manner, you can expect explosive growth throughout the Kingdom of God.

But remember: an understanding of the big picture is what keeps you on track. That understanding will keep things in perspective and help you stay on the right track to evangelism or discipleship.

Then dream those Holy Ghost dreams. Dream them big. Find the place in which you can pursue your vision. Be faithful to the larger vision, not using it as a stepping-stone, and God's plan for you will progress rapidly.

18

MANAGEMENT BY OBJECTIVES

God has anointed us to lead, to impart direction to others. However, if we ignore the practical aspects of leadership, such as administration and management, no matter how strong the anointing on our lives is, we will never succeed as leaders.

There are a lot of different management philosophies in the world which teach how to direct the behavior of employees to produce the desired result. The one I think is most in line with Scripture is a concept called management by objective. Every level of leadership in an organization can implement this management philosophy.

An organizational flowchart is a pyramid of authority. One person is at the top, and he or she is the final authority in that organization. There can be only one head. Similarly, the Bible teaches that God leads through one Head: He is Jesus.

While there is only one head, that person does not do everything himself. Some authority must be delegated. On every level of management, beginning at the top, the one in charge must have others he can rely on to carry out his vision. A leader is most effective with only eight or ten people reporting directly to him. If he is to speak into their lives, he has to know them, build that trust level with them so he flows with them, investing in them the leadership principles which will cause them to grow.

Then each of those people should ideally have eight, ten or twelve people beneath them. And each of those people should also have eight, ten or twelve people beneath them. No matter how big the organization, through this pyramid you can maintain a flow of direction through every individual.

Conversely, the pyramid structure provides a connection for accountability. Everyone has to be accountable to a higher authority.

Goals and Objectives

Habakkuk 2:2 says, **Write the vision, and make it plain upon tables, that he may run that readeth it.** The next step is to bring this grand vision, the dream God has placed on your heart, down to a meaningful set of goals and objectives that you can pursue and measure. It won't do you any good to have a wonderful Holy Ghost vision in your heart about where you are to go and what you are to do if you have no intermediate goals and objectives to make the vision meaningful to your daily activity. This is also true for the people who work for you. If they cannot relate the things they are doing to the big picture by achieving goals and objectives, then they are not going to be motivated to continue achieving them.

Remember, it is vision that produces behavior. If someone cannot see that what he or she is doing relates to a larger purpose and is contributing to the success of the endeavor, then his or her behavior is going to be inconsistent.

THE MARK, THE PRIZE AND THE HIGH CALLING

Hebrews 11:6 tells us that in order to please God we must have faith. That faith consists not only of believing that God is but that He is a rewarder. The Lord has made us to be motivated by a prize. That prize is a higher quality of life, the God kind of life, which we're to pursue until we reach our ultimate high calling and then go home to be with the Lord. The closer we move in harmony with the revealed will of God and His destiny for our lives, the higher quality of life we will have and the more of the prize we are going to experience.

But Paul says in Philippians 3:14 that we do not press toward either the prize or the high calling. We press toward *the mark* of the prize.

Now, *to press* means "to make a strong, consistent effort."[1] You can be motivated by the prize, but it is not what orients your effort. Many people orient all of their efforts toward healing or prosperity or some other promise of God that is *part* of the prize. But you are not to press toward that. You are not to make it the focal point of what you do and expend your effort toward. That may be your motivation, but you press toward the mark, not the prize or the high calling.

The lofty destiny God has given you is probably a little too fuzzy a concept for you to know exactly how to proceed in order to arrive at that point. So there is a mark you press toward.

The high calling is the long-range goal. That is the ultimate place you believe God has called you to be. But there are intermediate marks which are intended to take you in the direction of the high call and which provide you with a means to measure your progress.

HITTING YOUR MARKS

Bowling is a pretty good example of this principle because you have pins down at the far end of the alley and a set of marks where you put your feet just before you release the ball. Theoretically, if you make exactly the same approach to the marks and release the ball the same way every time and roll the ball toward a particular spot, you will get a strike. The marks make the process a whole lot easier than simply looking down at the pins and trying to get the ball to go where you want it to go.

The "mark" of Philippians 3:14 operates in much the same way. When you orient your life toward that mark, you win the prize. Now, some of the marks God gives you in the Scriptures are marks of love, marks of service to other people, marks which keep you oriented toward the high calling of God.

But, aside from the Word, God will speak things to your heart which are intermediate goals to take you toward that high calling. As you sit before the Lord, thinking about your life in ministry and praying in the Holy Spirit, pray about the intermediate marks that you are to press toward right now. God may have shown you that your high calling is to preach to hundreds of thousands of people in huge stadiums all over the world. But right now He has set a mark for you which involves your job at a particular ministry or in a particular vocation, and that mark will take you in the direction you are going to go some day. It is an intermediate mark for you.

If You Carry the Vision

As a manager, a pastor or an entrepreneur, you should be praying about the goals for that year which are going to take your organization toward the mark. You will have to put these goals into meaningful terms for those who work for you, so your goals will become the way you set marks for others in various areas of your organization. As everybody makes their effort toward their mark, the result will be the organization reaching its mark for the year.

This year our ministry has a mark of getting 100,000 confirmed salvations. We have many different departments which contribute to that mark. Our missions department has sixteen short-term missions trips this year into other countries. Our evangelism department schedules street witnessing every week, and the children's ministry has a "Backyard Bible Church" outreach during the summer, to name a few. Each department has different marks which contribute to the overall church mark of 100,000.

We have an attendance goal of 8,000, and again, whether it is the ushers, the greeters or the small group ministry, many different departments make their contributions toward reaching that mark. Each one's goals, objectives and marks will come together to produce the church mark.

> *Each one's goals, objectives and marks will come together to produce the church mark.*

We have a financial mark for the year, and there are a lot of different ways income is generated. General fund contributions, restricted fund contributions, book and tape sales, tuition—all of these are different ways income is generated in the ministry. And all of these contribute to hitting the overall financial mark we have set for the coming year.

Sit down with the people who work for you and help them establish marks they can press toward. Make their individual marks a meaningful contribution to the overall organizational mark for that year. Doing so will give them a sense of ownership of the mark they are corporately reaching toward, and it will motivate them to maximize their efforts.

DEALING WITH ASSOCIATES

When I begin planning for an upcoming budget year, I sit down with each of my associate pastors and we negotiate a mark for his area of responsibility for the coming year. I say negotiate because it is important that he have a part in this process, as he is the one responsible for hitting the mark.

I will tell him what I believe is a realistic church mark for the year. Then we will discuss his department mark and how it contributes to the overall church mark. When each department hits their mark, all these marks add up to the church's mark and we have progressed toward the long-range goal and objective God has given us: the high calling.

But my associates must each have a mark meaningful to him, and he must see his part as important. I must communicate to him the importance of his contribution, and he must communicate with me what he thinks he can do. How high is he willing to reach? Where can he set his mark?

I may also have to set more than one mark for each person with whom I am negotiating. There may be a financial mark as well as a production mark, but each of these marks is a result of the process of negotiation.

Then during the course of the year, I meet with each associate and we talk about progress toward the mark. I ask him how it's going because I am a resource to him. If he is having a problem reaching his mark, I am there to provide what help I can. If I see that he is not making the mark, I must be ready to admonish or encourage him.

Sometimes you will have to encourage your associates because some people are a little bit bashful about setting the mark too high; you have to push them up a little bit. Other times you may realize that they are being a little unrealistic, so you will have to bring them back down to earth. The bottom line is you don't want them to get blown out by failure.

THE PRIZE

Your challenge as a leader is to shrink what is big (the vision) down to the manageable (goals and objectives). You must reduce the large vision down to the daily undertakings which take you in that direction. It takes thought on the part of everyone who stands in a role of leadership in an organization. From the senior pastor or the administrator of a business or ministry, to the department heads and section leaders, each leader must ask him- or herself, "How am I going to put these goals into meaningful terms my people can grasp and carry out on a daily basis?"

You must have a plan.

I can remember very clearly the first day I shared God's vision for our ministry with our congregation. The church had been started only a month and a half earlier, and I was firmly impressed with the need to let people know we had a purpose and a direction. It was glorious because it had come from the Holy Spirit. But it was also so grand that, in natural terms, it was not very manageable.

What I had seen in my heart was a sanctuary with 15,000 seats. That meant a congregation of approximately 40,000 people. I had also seen other things such as a retirement home complex and a hospice to minister to the terminally ill in an environment filled with faith. All of these things were out of our reach at that point. I mean, there we were, a month and a half into this, and I really had some God-sized dreams! A person had to wonder how you even begin proceeding down that path.

As I said, I felt a real need to share the vision with my congregation. So there I was, sharing this with a congregation of twenty-five people! I was telling them about a 15,000-seat sanctuary and a retirement home and a hospice, and I just know they were thinking, *Isn't he cute.* But I knew I needed to put it out there. The Bible says you have to make the vision plain.

Well, with only twenty-five people we were a long way from a 15,000 seat sanctuary; we were in a conference room in the hotel theater.

So what do you do to bring such a huge vision down to something you can do now, something manageable? What will meaningfully launch you in that direction?

GETTING STARTED

Obviously, intermediate growth has to occur first. If you are going to get to 15,000 people, you have to be at ten first, and you had to be at five before that. Well, a number which was manageable for those twenty-five people was about 300 to 400 people. That number was a believable or reachable goal for a small group just starting a church. So I revised my first figure and said our first goal was to have three to four hundred people.

Now what kind of facility would accommodate that number of people? We looked around and found one in the local community college. It had an auditorium we could rent for a reasonable amount.

This was shrinking the big dream to something manageable, then setting intermediate goals and objectives which would provide us with a plan of action to take us in the direction of the 15,000.

I firmly believe God validates the rightness or the wrongness of our direction by providential circumstance. If we had gone to that community college and been unable to rent their auditorium, that would have indicated to me that no door was open and we were looking in the wrong direction. I would have realized we needed to try somewhere else. But when you are following the leading of the Holy Spirit, you can expect Him to make a way for you. The college had never allowed churches to use their facilities prior to that time, but they allowed us to and they have since that time. God opened that door for us.

So at that time we had only twenty-five people, and we had just rented a 300-seat auditorium. We had enough financial resources among us to rent the auditorium for two months. We took a step of faith and moved over there.

Something else figured into our scenario. I could not pastor full-time with only twenty-five people. I had to continue to operate my air freight business at that point. But I also knew I could not build our fellowship to 15,000 people as a part-time pastor. So somehow I had to plan the transition from the business into the ministry. I also had to make sure the ministry was going to be able to support my family's needs so I didn't have to reduce our standard of living, as I did well in business.

This is the way God spoke to me about it. The ministry is not a demotion; it is a promotion which flows into every area of your life, including finances. If I could trust Him for the vision, I could trust Him for the provision. So we began to move ahead with our plans.

Now, that's just an example of how to manage by objectives. Remember, you set a mark, and then you press toward it. Essentially, you're pressing toward God's high calling for your life.

19

GETTING YOUR GAME PLAN

After setting realistic objectives, your next step is to devise a meaningful game plan. It will be different for everyone. I cannot do this for you; however, I can use my experience as an example of how conceptually you can bring a magnificent dream down to a manageable beginning.

When we started our church, we had an auditorium which would seat 300 people, and we had enough money to rent it for eight weeks. I wanted to devote my effort to the full-time pursuit of ministry, so my immediate goal was 125 people. The Lord provided that opportunity very quickly. Through a merger with another church, our membership went immediately to more than 125 people.

On the basis of the offerings we were receiving at that point, I was able to exit from my business, go into the ministry full-time and expect to maintain the same standard of living.

How do you reach that first level, whether it's 25 or 125? Well, you have to let people know you are there. You have to let people know you are the best thing happening in that area of town, the Word is being preached and by the power of the Holy Spirit lives are being changed.

How do you do that? Evangelize, share your faith. Perhaps distribute a few door hangers in the neighborhood to let them know you are there. Formulate a plan to spread the word about the church and then involve the people who are a part of the fellowship in the efforts. The fruit of our efforts was to fill that 300-seat sanctuary, which would enable us to move to the second step—a 1,500-seat sanctuary in a warehouse complex.

Break the goals down into intermediate objectives realistic enough to encourage church members' participation. They will then see the fruit of their effort producing progress toward their goal. We did this for a number of different areas of the ministry, breaking down each part of the vision for our church into manageable and reachable goals.

NEGOTIATING THE ANNUAL REVIEW

On a predetermined schedule, usually annually, the leader of every department or ministry must schedule time with each person who works for him or her. During those meetings, the leader brings the ministry objective down to meaningful intermediate goals and objectives.

For example, if you run the mail room, spend time with each of the people who work there. Talk about the impact of the ministry and how it is extended to the people who write in, the result of the seed they plant, where it goes, what it does, how sowing impacts their life and so forth. Discuss how their contribution enables you to reach your intermediate and long-range goals. Describe their job in terms of those goals and objectives which contribute to the overall ministry effort so their job keeps from becoming just a task they can easily grow weary of. Help them understand the importance of the part they play in the overall picture.

Remember, though, this is a negotiating session. Why? Because you are interested in having them share what is in their hearts. You want them not only to acknowledge your direction to their work, but you want them to say, "Well, this is what I think. I have an idea. Maybe we could do this, and hopefully it would produce these results."

You want them to expand the gifts in them and pursue the vision God has given them. If you have staffed correctly and the people can actually realize their vision within the larger framework of the ministry's vision, then your department is going to grow by letting God use the gifts in those people.

At this point you can tell them how the overall ministry goals and objectives dictate what their production must be. Tell them what fruit you want to see. Ask for their agreement and discuss whether or not this fruit will move their area of ministry toward the overall goals. Ask them if this fruit is something they can agree with and be a part of, and, if so, ask them if they have any new ideas to increase productivity. Let them outline a plan for you about how they are going to do what they propose. Make sure they understand what the plan means in terms of the effort they have to invest.

This process should take at least a couple of sessions, and it should be informal. Remember, leadership is relationship. Be transparent and open. Maybe you could discuss it over lunch, but do not make it a session in which you dictate. Let the gifts in them begin to flow, because that is what ultimately will benefit your goals and objectives. And the more they contribute at this stage, the more solid the measurement parameter is for the reward system, which makes management by objective so effective.

THE PRIZE

What motivates people? Motivation has been studied for decades by the best minds in the secular world. The consensus is that the best way to keep somebody motivated is to have a reward system which incorporates praise and recognition, in addition to monetary rewards in the form of raises or bonuses.

They are right. It should not surprise you that this approach is scriptural. God says the laborer is worthy of his hire. (Luke 10:7.) That means you should pay him for what he does and pay him well. So management by objective incorporates this concept of reward.

ACTIVATING THE REWARD

Once you have brought the vision down to an objective everyone can handle and you have negotiated a plan for pursuing that objective, you have activated the reward system you have put in place. Then all along the way, the verbal praise and recognition keeps the wheels turning until you reach the point of giving a monetary reward on the basis of an annual performance review. You are letting them run with their vision, what is in their hearts. They have said this is a meaningful goal for them to shoot for. They have said this is how they want to pursue it. Now they are rewarded for the fruit produced, both by recognition and by monetary reward.

Now, during the course of the year, you do not just ignore them. Don't just talk to them once or twice a year and then go back the next year and take an account. You must be a resource to them in the accomplishment of their goals and objectives. Whatever encouragement or exhortation is required, whatever technical skill or ability you can lend to them when they have a problem, you are a resource to them in pursuit of the goals and objectives which you have helped them negotiate. During the course of the year, make yourself readily available on a frequent basis for that purpose.

STAFFING FOR VISION

Let's say you are a department head who has responsibility for negotiating and remaining within certain budgetary parameters. You have finances allocated to your department, and part of your management responsibility is to maintain that budget. Something you need to be aware of in regard to recommendations and budgetary provision for staffing is that you should hire staff for the vision and not for the need.

Most of the time, our mentality is to wait until we are squeezed to the point that everyone is working sixty hours a week; then we add one more person before we collapse and die. That is totally self-defeating; it promotes burnout. No one can go 100 miles an hour indefinitely and maintain his enthusiasm about what he is doing. To accommodate growth without burning everyone out, you are going to have to staff for the vision. That process should be part of the negotiating process during the annual objective and goal setting.

> *To accommodate growth without burning everyone out, you are going to have to staff for the vision.*

Then part of the negotiating process should make room for the budgetary allowances which will be necessary in order to add additional staff when you achieve your vision. Make that allowance before you ever reach that point.

Also, when you staff, make sure you match people's vision and the gifts that are a part of their vision with their job description. The most successful businesses put people where they love to work, doing the things they really like to do. So whether it is at the time of the initial staffing or when someone is promoted within an organization, do so in line with their gifting.

Sometimes a person is a good worker and he makes a healthy contribution doing a certain job, so he gets promoted without much regard to his gifts. Then he is like a fish out of water. He doesn't do as well in his new job because he has gotten out of line with his gifting. People perform best where their heart is and where their gifts are. That is always revealed by desire.

You should ask the people who work for you what their greatest desire is regarding their labor in ministry. Then to the greatest extent possible, align that desire with their job description.

MANAGEMENT BY OBJECTIVE IN SCRIPTURE

I mentioned earlier that Scripture is full of examples of management by objective. Let's look at Philippians 3:13-14.

Brethren, I count not myself to have apprehended: but this one thing I do, forgetting those things which are behind, and reaching forth unto those things which are before, I press toward the mark for the prize of the high calling of God in Christ Jesus.

Verse 14 is a scriptural rendering of management by objective: **I press toward the mark for the prize of the high calling of God in Christ Jesus.** The high calling of God in Christ Jesus for our lives is the Lord's divinely appointed destiny for each one of us: His perfect will, His plan, His highest and His best for us.

Paul is saying, "That is where I'm going. I'm going toward the high calling of God in Christ Jesus." But he does not say he presses toward the high calling. That is too lofty, too hard to define, too hard to see how you will get there. How can you press toward something that is almost beyond imagination? There has to be an intermediate mark. It is the mark which Paul presses toward. That is the intermediate goal and objective. He does not press toward the high calling (the vision itself); he presses toward the mark (the goals and objectives) of the high calling.

And there is a reward when you get there. A prize! That is what Scripture says—"press toward the mark." Why? You must press to receive the prize of the high calling of God in Christ Jesus. This is another scriptural support of the truth that it is appropriate to motivate by reward and reward incorporates material remuneration.

THE HIGH CALLING

What is the high calling of God? It is God's perfect will for your life. Is there any poverty or lack in God's perfect will for your life? No. God's perfect will for your life incorporates a divine provision which He describes as all sufficient in all things, according to His riches in glory by Christ Jesus. (Phil. 4:19.) So, part of the prize for our arriving where God wants us to be is financial or material remuneration.

Paul says he is motivated by that prize in his press toward intermediate goals and objectives. He said he was pressing toward the mark. Why? Just because philosophically it is the right thing to do? No! He presses toward the mark for the prize because it carries an increased quality of life. It carries a reward with it, and God made us to respond to a reward system.

Pressing toward the mark means the expenditure of effort. If your people are going to meaningfully expend effort to accomplish the desired end, you must have intermediate goals and objectives which will take them toward the high calling or the long-range vision and purpose for the ministry which God has put in your heart. The intermediate goals and objectives are what make it possible to press, and what motivate people to continue expending effort is the certainty of reward. So we have Paul's rendering of management by objective, a scriptural system which hinges on having a clear vision.

BRING REALITY TO YOUR VISION

It all starts with vision. You understand the big picture, what the primary reason for ministry is, what your dispensational mandate is. Then you boil that down to your individual calling, the vision God has given you. You find a ministry within which your vision can fit and see the highest fulfillment of that vision within the framework of a larger ministry's vision.

Then as you are promoted up the leadership ladder, you do the same for the people who work for you, being sure, as much as possible, to give them the latitude to pursue their vision. Again, this is within the framework of the overall ministry vision.

To do this effectively, you must bring the vision down to manageable, intermediate goals and objectives which those under you can become part of through the process of negotiation, during which you formulate a plan with them.

Based on how well they meet the negotiated goals and objectives, they are rewarded for their efforts both with recognition and finances. Through this entire process you are a resource to help or encourage them in their pursuit of the vision.

That is management by objective, and it works on every level of leadership because it is scriptural. It carries with it, therefore, the supernatural ability of God. It will produce the results you desire in your life.

20

MANAGING COMPLEXITY

Once you become that relational leader that we've been talking about and people desire to follow you, one of the biggest challenges you'll face is dealing with that inevitable byproduct of growth—complexity. This is where leadership at a high level really becomes crucial.

Once God has brought you the crew or troop He wants you to lead, your challenge then is to make the right decisions that take you down a path of increase for your life and for your organization.

Like it or not, for each of us life is a constant stream of decisions. But as a leader, you must make decisions that affect many other people. And as your organization grows, those decisions become increasingly important and increasingly complex. So the challenge for the leader is managing ever-increasing complexity.

There have been many articles written in the secular business arena about the matter of managing complexity. Ten years ago, Professor Elliott Jacques published an excellent article in Harvard Business

Review which dealt with this very subject.[1] Much of what he wrote was consistent with Scripture, and it made me wonder if this guy had done a little reading in the Word of God on the side!

The ability of a leader to manage complexity is ultimately what limits the growth or increase of a corporate organization. When a leader's capacity to manage complexity is reached, growth stops.

There are a variety of things that affect complexity, such as the numbers of variables, people and time frames involved. As the organization grows, the decision becomes more complex, and it becomes more of a challenge to make right decisions and, therefore, make progress down the path of God's will for your life.

THE IMPORTANCE OF STRUCTURE

How do you manage increasing complexity in a growing organization? One of the most important keys is providing the right structure. Without proper organizational structure, it is impossible to deal with complexity.

Most organizations establish their levels of authority based on pay raises and longevity. This occurs when an organization grows. When an employee has been with you for a year or two, you establish another level of authority in order to give him a pay raise that accommodates his longevity or seniority. When you operate this way, you wind up establishing levels of authority on the basis of longevity and the need to give somebody a pay raise rather than for valid structural reasons.

This leads to too many layers of bureaucracy and an organizational pyramid that is too steep. Levels of management should be a direct reflection of the levels of complexity of the tasks and roles.

Even with the proper structure, your capacity to deal with complexity is still a limiting factor. How do you increase your capacity to manage complexity?

The secular answer to this question is through the educational process. And there is a kernel of biblical truth in this view. God's Word tells us that knowledge is important. (Fools hate knowledge, according to Proverbs 1:22.) It's a spiritual cop-out to say, "Well, the anointing will accomplish everything I need to accomplish."

If you're interested in growing to the maximum capacity you have in God, you're going to have to increase what He has to work with. You should always be learning. Some sort of schooling is a healthy thing for everybody. It doesn't have to be formal, however. You don't have to be enrolled in the college downtown. Formal education is a wonderful thing if it is available to you, but however you do it, learning and expanding your knowledge base is a direct contributor to your ability to handle complexity.

A WORKOUT FOR YOUR MIND

Another factor that, according to much of the secular world, aids in increasing your ability to handle complexity is the exercise of your mental capacities. As you do hard analytical work—as you go through the logical processes that bring you to valid conclusions—you're increasing your mental faculties.

Do as much reading as you can. Be widely read, not only for the purpose of acquiring relevant knowledge but also for stimulating thought.

Challenge your mind. Work problems and solve puzzles. Problem-solving is an excellent method of exercising that gray matter between your ears. And *exercise* is the right word. Your brain is just like a muscle. If it lies dormant too long, it gets weak.

I believe there are far too many people in the body of Christ who have said, "Well, it's the Lord, and it's the anointing. So I don't need training or education." This is wrong thinking and unfortunate. You must give God something to work with. Of course, He does use the foolish things of the world—I'm an example of that! But that doesn't mean you have to stay willfully ignorant.

THE SUPERNATURAL EDGE

As we've seen, the need to expand your capacity to manage complexity does have some natural considerations: keeping your mind active, reading as much as you can, continuing to gather knowledge and fostering the learning process all of your life. Making a commitment to never stop learning. These are all natural considerations that believers and non-believers alike can utilize to better manage complexity.

But, fortunately for the believer, we have more than natural strategies at our disposal. The Bible gives us a supernatural edge over people in the world, as far as managing complexity is concerned.

Look, for example, at Psalm 119:130:

The entrance of thy words giveth light; it giveth understanding unto the simple.

When you look up the Hebrew word translated *simple* in the concordance, you find two possible meanings.[2] One is "foolish." That's what we think of when we read this: God's words give understanding—to the guy who isn't all there.

Of course, the Word of God certainly can give such a person some light and understanding, but that's not the message I get from this verse.

You see, the other possible meaning for this Hebrew word is "uncomplicated." That would make our reading of the verse: "The entrance of thy words giveth light; it gives understanding unto the *uncomplicated.*"

This gives us a powerful incentive to manage complexity. God gives special wisdom and insight to those who simplify their lives.

When you violate the principles in God's Word, life gets very complicated very quickly. Conversely, following the Word of God tends to uncomplicate your life. In other words, applying the Word of God to every facet of life has the effect of helping you manage complexity.

Let us now extend this truth to the realm of leadership.

SIMPLIFYING DECISIONS

Complexity is having more variables, more factors and more information flying at you as you try to make decisions. One of the keys to effective decision-making as things begin to become more complex is to pare away the trivial issues until you get to the core. Then your decision is much more likely to be a good one.

You may have a challenge that looks so tangled and so complex that making a sound decision seems impossible. But as you begin to ask, "What's really the issue here? What's this all about?" things begin to come into focus.

Of course, this is a technique even unbelievers can utilize. Those of us who are born-again, however, can utilize the power of the Spirit and the Word in determining what's relevant and what's extraneous. And what a difference it makes!

On many occasions I have looked at a leadership challenge and said, "Boy, this is a tough one." But I started praying about the matter in the Holy Spirit.

Romans 8:26, 27 tells us what happens when we pray in the Holy Ghost:

Likewise the Spirit also helpeth our infirmities: for we know not what we should pray for as we ought: but the Spirit itself maketh intercession for us with groanings which cannot be uttered. And he that searcheth the hearts knoweth what is the mind of the Spirit, because he maketh intercession for the saints according to the will of God.

You may not know how to pray as you ought, but the Spirit makes intercession for you according to the will of God. And it says in 1 Corinthians 2:13 that those who possess the Holy Spirit will be able to interpret spiritual things:

Which things also we speak, not in the words which man's wisdom teacheth, but which the Holy Ghost teacheth; comparing spiritual things with spiritual.

So as you're praying in the Holy Ghost and considering an issue that seems very complex, God will give you a word. He'll give you a thought. He'll give you an idea. Then you can meditate on it. That's His testimony to you regarding that problem.

Suddenly a problem that had seemed very complex and intractable now seems simple. It has happened this way for me on countless occasions. And God's no respecter of persons. It can happen for you that way too. This is the way the Bible says it's supposed to happen, because He simplifies the complicated. His Word brings light and understanding.

TAKING THE NEXT STEP

It's one thing to make a decision. It's another thing to see that decision implemented. It's one thing to decide that point "B" is your destination. It's another thing to know what route you need to take to get there.

Complexity exists in both arenas. Decision-making involves mental processes. Implementation requires a plan. And complexity can make both difficult.

How do you manage the complexities that come with implementation? We see an example of how to do this in the sixth chapter of Acts:

And in those days, when the number of the disciples was multiplied, there arose a murmuring of the Grecians against the Hebrews, because their widows were neglected in the daily ministration. Then the twelve called the multitude of the disciples unto them, and said, It is not reason that we should leave the word of God, and serve tables. Wherefore, brethren, look ye out among you seven men of honest report, full of the Holy Ghost and wisdom, whom we may appoint over this business. But we will give ourselves continually to prayer, and to the ministry of the word.

And the saying pleased the whole multitude: and they chose Stephen, a man full of faith and of the Holy Ghost, and Philip, and Prochorus, and Nicanor, and Timon, and Parmenas, and Nicolas a proselyte of Antioch: Whom they set before the apostles: and when they had prayed, they laid their hands on them. And the word of God increased; and the number of the disciples multiplied in Jerusalem greatly; and a great company of the priests were obedient to the faith.

Acts 6:1-7

There are some important leadership truths here. The apostles were faced with a potentially complex situation. This wasn't an insignificant issue, or it wouldn't be recorded in the Bible. No, this was potentially a divisive and significant event in the life of the early Church.

Here we see the apostle managing a potentially complex situation properly. As a result, the Bible tells us the Word of God increased, the number of the disciples multiplied and a great many priests were obedient to the faith. (v. 7.)

But the potential complexity in this situation came from more than just the need to minister to the widows. It not only involved the handling of money, but sensitive ethnic issues as well. You have a potentially incendiary situation here.

The fact is, money is always a powder-keg issue.

What was the key to implementing God's wisdom in this case? One important word—*delegation*. Complex implementation becomes simple through the proper use of delegation. You must be willing to delegate.

This is one of the most common causes of under-achievement and failure I see. On many occasions I've seen business owners, managers and even pastors who can't or won't let go of responsibilities. They're convinced nobody can do it any better than they. So they hold on.

But as growth comes and complexity increases, leaders such as these become swamped, paralyzed and ineffective. Growth stops and often reverses.

You will reach a point in your growth curve at which it is no longer appropriate for you to do a lot of the things that you handled in the past.

At that point you must rise to the highest level of leadership: You must develop other leaders around you. When you delegate, you're engaging the purest form of leadership development by developing those beneath you. You're giving them an opportunity to grow.

This is how the complexity of implementation is managed. As you do it, people around you are growing. Your time is protected. And you're able to focus on the things only you can do—things like developing and sharing the vision.

You see, at the end of the day, your responsibility as leader is to be the strategist. To see the big picture. To do the thinking. Somebody has to be able to see the forest and the trees. Somebody has to pray and spend time with the Lord. As a leader, that somebody is you.

SIMPLIFY

This is how God intends us to manage complexity. We must master the two-part consideration: decision-making and implementation.

First, you must give God an opportunity to speak to you. He'll begin to bring understanding to you as you pare away the irrelevant. Once you're able to see the core issue, you can make the right decision.

Then in implementing, you must look for ways to delegate. This gives you the time to get alone with God and hear from Him again. And the cycle continues.

It's a cycle of growth and increase, a cycle of upward fulfillment of God's plan and destiny. It's a cycle called leadership.

SECTION 3

The Successful Communicator

21

COMMUNICATING YOUR VISION

The second vital area of focus for successful leadership is communication. No matter how clearly you have heard from God about the direction for your life and the vision for your calling, if you cannot communicate it to other people, it stops right there. It dies unborn inside you.

For a leader, the ability to communicate effectively is one of the most important skills to develop. Oftentimes we view effective communication as a product of personality or gifting. And that is not true. No one is born with a silver tongue. No one automatically has all it takes to be a gifted communicator. It is something you learn and deliberately cultivate.

Anything meaningful which happens in your life involves relationships, and successful conduct in those relationships depends on your ability to communicate clearly and in a way that will inspire and motivate others. Communication is, without a doubt, one of the most important things for any person to develop if they are interested in succeeding in life. And for a leader it is an absolute essential.

PLACING A PREMIUM ON COMMUNICATION

Put a premium on the ability to communicate well. Make a decision that you are going to allow the Lord to shape your communication skills in a way that will enable you to be more effective as a leader. Nothing has a greater impact on that effectiveness than your ability to communicate.

The Bible says we must become good communicators if we are going to accurately share our vision and give direction to the goals God has set before us. Therefore, it is important that we know how communication takes place. What happens? How do we communicate things to another person?

TWO LEVELS OF COMMUNICATION

There are basically two levels of communication. One is verbal communication and the other is nonverbal communication. Let's take a look at what the Word has to say about communication from these two perspectives. God gives us a lot of specifics.

Let no corrupt communication proceed out of your mouth, but that which is good to the use of edifying, that it may minister grace unto the hearers.

Ephesians 4:29

The word *corrupt* does not mean cursing or slang or profanity. The Greek word for *corrupt* means "worthless."[1] You could read that verse like this: "Let no worthless communication proceed out of your mouth."

The next part of that verse defines *worthless* by telling us that if our communication is not edifying, it is worthless. Now the Greek word for edify means "to build up," as in building up the Kingdom of God or the body of Christ.[2]

So Ephesians 4:29 is telling us that the words that come out of our mouths are worthless if they do not build up the Kingdom or the Body. That is why Jesus said we will be accountable for every idle word we speak.

MINISTERING GRACE

Not only must our words build up the Kingdom and the Body, they must **minister grace unto the hearers,** or as the Phillips translation puts it, we must speak words **which God can use to help other people.** That is the kind of communication that should come from our mouths—words God can use to help other people. What is one way God helps other people? By using what we say to give them direction for their lives.

> *Not only must our words build up the Kingdom and the Body, they must minister grace unto the hearers . . .*

In James 3:4-5 he likens the tongue to a rudder on a ship.

Behold also the ships, which though they be so great, and are driven of fierce winds, yet are they turned about with a very small helm [rudder].... Even so the tongue is a little member.... Behold, how great a matter a little fire kindleth!

Huge ships are given direction by the comparatively little rudder; the same is true in the issues of this life. Groups of people are given direction by one little tongue. It is a powerful member.

God is going to use your tongue, or Satan is going to use your tongue. God is going to use your tongue to direct people and build up the body of Christ, or Satan is going to use your tongue to tear down the body of Christ. It's going to be one or the other.

Paul makes a similar point in Ephesians 5:6: **Let no man deceive you with vain words.** That Greek word *vain* means nearly the same thing as *corrupt*. It means empty. In other words, Paul is saying, let no man deceive you with empty, worthless words. Do you want to know how to avoid being deceived? Do not listen to anything that does not build up or edify the body of Christ. If you want to get drawn into deception, if you want to be one of those people 2 Timothy 4:3 says has itching ears, then listen to vain or empty words.

OTHER FORMS OF COMMUNICATION

There are other forms of communication as well. The apostle Paul says every sound on the face of this earth has some significance. (1 Cor. 14:10.) Every sound has a meaning and is a form of communication.

There are a lot of questions my wife, Lynne, can ask me, and I just grunt in response. But she understands me. We all know men have different grunts for different things. And likewise, she communicates verbally with me without using words, and I know what she means. Sometimes she will just say, "Whew," and I know that means "I've had it. I'm going to bed." A lot of our communication is not verbal.

NONVERBAL COMMUNICATION

For our gospel came not unto you in word only, but also in power, and in the Holy Ghost, and in much assurance [How is it able to come that way? Because] **...ye know what manner of men we were among you for your sake. And ye became followers of us, and of the Lord, having received the word in much affliction, with joy of the Holy Ghost: So that ye were ensamples to all that believe in Macedonia and Achaia.**

1 Thessalonians 1:5-7

What brought the gospel to the Thessalonians, not in word only, but in the Holy Ghost and in power and in assurance? The nonverbal example of Paul's life was confirmation of the Word he preached. It is a basic Bible premise. Faith without action is dead. There has to be a corresponding action to your words of faith.

The church at Thessalonica followed Paul's example, and as a result, they became examples themselves. Why? Because Paul lived what he preached; his life was an example to the believers. That example put power into his words and gave assurance to the people affected by his ministry that what he said was right, and it worked.

There are many other forms of nonverbal communication, such as touch or facial expressions. But the principle form of nonverbal communication for a believer is the example you set by the way you live your life.

This principle of our lives being effective nonverbal communication is reflected many places in Scripture. Peter tells the elders among him who feed the flock of God to be examples to the flock. (1 Peter 5:1-3.)

Paul exhorts Timothy, as a young pastor, to be an example to the believers. Then he tells him how: **In word, in conversation, in charity, in spirit, in faith, in purity** (1 Tim. 4:12).

The writer of Hebrews tells us to be followers of those who through faith and patience inherit the promises. (Heb. 6:12.)

Additionally, we are to follow the faith of those who have the rule (governing authority) over us—**Whose faith follow, considering the end of their conversation** (Heb. 13:7). In other words, if they are practicing what they preach and it is producing fruit in their life, follow their faith.

FOLLOWING EXAMPLES

When we talk about following the example of a man, it is with the knowledge that every man is subject to mistakes. So ultimately we look to Jesus; He is our measuring stick. The Word of God, both living and written, is our measuring stick.

But many baby Christians and immature believers have not developed any spiritual eyesight yet. They can't see Jesus, so they have to have a physical example to follow until they have matured to a point where they can see Jesus. Baby Christians and immature believers are just like children in the natural.

For a natural child, the first seven or eight years of his life, his parents are his life. Everything they do is an example to that child. As the child gets a little older, he starts looking around and getting input from other areas, his peers, TV, books.

It is the same in the realm of the spirit. When you are separated to leadership, you have to be an example because a lot of babes in Christ are going to be looking at you. No matter how often you say, "Look unto Jesus, He's the One," they are going to see your example, and it will impart direction to them.

Are you convinced of the importance of effective communication? Has that been planted firmly in your heart? Verbal and nonverbal communication is vital to your success as a leader. But knowing that still isn't enough; you've got to learn effective communication skills and put them into practice.

22

DISTORTED COMMUNICATION

On the pathway of learning effective communication skills, the biggest obstacle is yet ahead of you, because there are literally thousands of ways in which communication is distorted. A leader has a huge challenge set before him. He has to take the vision God has given him and transmit it via word and example to the people who are his responsibility. His communication must cause the vision to be duplicated in their minds as accurately as possible, because it is that vision which their faith puts substance to. All this must be accomplished, losing as little as possible in the transmission, if the corporate Body is to do what God wants it to do.

Communication is distorted in many ways. If you are in a hurry and you do not give someone all the information they need, then you have painted an incorrect picture in their minds. Your communication has been flawed.

Or if someone isn't paying attention to what you are saying because they are preoccupied with other things, communication has been distorted. The wrong image has been painted on their minds.

The environment can also affect communication. If someone has two little kids crying and pulling on his leg, the phone is ringing and a pot on the stove just boiled over, do you think you are going to be able to effectively communicate what you need? Most likely not. You will only have misunderstanding.

Ethnic and cultural backgrounds can distort not only what we hear but what we say, because certain gestures and words may mean one thing to some people and something totally different to others. That's another way communication can become distorted.

DISTRUST, THE 'BIGGIE'

But here is the biggie—the biggest thing which distorts communication: distrust. Distrust keeps you from receiving what is being said to you as truth; it causes you to have a totally inaccurate interpretation of what is being communicated to you. Distrust can cause you to pick up an offense when there was none implied. Often before the communication can be clarified, the offense must be forgiven. Because communication is such a fragile thing, you must give some thought to your attitude.

If you do not feel well when you get out of bed in the morning, then pray yourself into a decent frame of mind before you go out the door or else stay at home. The way you deliver your message is important, so you will want as many things as possible working in your favor.

Many things contribute to effective delivery. Eye contact is one of them. Have you ever spoken with someone who cannot look you in the eyes? I just want to grab that person by the shirtfront and hold his head steady for a minute. I want to make him look at me or else know what he is hiding!

'I AIN'T NO ENGLISH MAJOR'

Being articulate is also important. Many people think it is cool to use a lot of colloquialisms and slang when, in fact, that will only undermine their credibility. People respect you when you are able to say what you want to say. And being articulate is nothing more than the result of a little awareness and a little practice.

Someone said to me once, "Well, I'm not an English major." That is not important. Focus on the importance of being articulate, not beating around the bush, not using a lot of slang and being concise. Then you will have a lot more credibility in people's minds than you would otherwise.

BE CLEAR, REPETITIVE AND CONGRUENT

Make your messages clear by being specific. A lot of people simply like to hear themselves talk. They give you so much information that you don't really know what their point is. They lose the impact of what they were saying. So be specific.

Secondly, be repetitive. Jesus was very redundant. He always got His message across at least twice. He would tell a parable and then He would explain the parable.

To send clear messages, we have to be specific and repetitive. And to keep the message from being confused, we have to be sure our verbal and our nonverbal communication is congruent. If I have a "don't mess with me" look on my face and say, "I love you," I have completely undermined the message I am sending.

Body language and personal hygiene can affect your communication as well. Have you ever talked to people who get right up in your face? They get into your personal space, and your walls go up—especially if they have bad breath. I can't even listen to what they are saying.

Every now and then you run into people who are standing in faith for something, and they will say, "I love you, brother," yet you know they hate your guts. What you do nonverbally has to be congruent with the verbal message you are sending.

SPEAKING THE TRUTH IN LOVE

One thing that must be foremost in our minds when we think of effective communication is how to speak the truth in love. (Eph. 4:15.) This concept more than anything else defines godly communication. It is on this basis of loving truth that right relationship is established, and God can then use you to bring ministry and blessing to the body of Christ. Speaking the truth in love is God's definition of effective communication.

As Christians, one of our concerns is to develop godly relationships in our lives. When you stop and think about it, nearly everything God has charged us to do in this life involves relationships.

In a discipling relationship, we establish a flow of God's Spirit through us to someone who needs to mature in His truths. We become instruments yielded to the Lord as ministers of reconciliation, helping to establish a relationship between a new believer and his newly found God.

In friendships, by the love of God that's been shed abroad in our hearts by the Holy Ghost, we establish relationships through which God can bring ministry to our lives, as well as ministry to the lives of others.

THE NINETY-NINE PERCENT REALITY

Do you realize that ninety-nine percent of what God does in your life will be through relationships? It is not wrong to envision the Lord's appearing in His glorified state to bring His will to pass in your life. But the truth of the matter is that if you need ministry or if you need to be encouraged or exhorted, it is far more likely that God will send somebody by to pat you on the back and say, "Cheer up. You are looking good!" rather than appearing in a little puffy cloud and saying, "Be thou encouraged, My child."

If He is going to meet your financial needs, He can certainly drop a sack of coins on your head from heaven, but it is far more likely that He will use someone to come to you and say, "I just had it on my heart to give you this."

God is going to use relationships, both to bring ministry to our lives and to enable us to minister to others. So if we have not taken care and made a deliberate effort to establish relationships, we have cut off channels of ministry from God to us and from God through us to someone else.

COMMUNICATION IN RELATIONSHIP

Now, the basis of any relationship—the vehicle by which love is communicated—and the thing that makes relationships possible is effective communication. If you love somebody but you are unable to communicate your love, you might as well not love him for all the good it will do. There will not be any relationship established on that love until you learn to communicate your love.

The ability to communicate effectively and thereby establish and maintain relationships, which enable God's ministry to flow in the earth today, is not a gift given to us when we come into the Kingdom of God. It is an acquired skill. Well, how do we acquire the skill? We turn to the Word of God.

RIGHT RELATIONSHIPS

God has much to say about making communication effective and, thereby, producing relationships He can use. Ephesians 4:16 says, **The**

whole body [is] fitly joined together and compacted by that which every joint supplieth, according to the effectual working in the measure of every part. Wouldn't you say this is a picture of the body of Christ when we are all in right relationship to one another?

In other words, members of the Body are going to be rightly related to one another on the basis of each member's supplying something to the relationship. Each member will supply something to the Body he or she is called to be a part of and also to other individual members of that body. There is a supply of time, a supply of gifts and effort, a supply of finances and a supply of love. And as every member makes his supply available, God says the Body is fitly joined together and right relationships result.

INCREASE OF THE BODY

This Scripture closes by saying the fruit of right relationships **maketh increase of the body unto the edifying of itself in love.** The result of right relationships is going to be increase for you individually as well as for us corporately as a church. If you have entered into right relationships, the result will be increase in your life: increase of God's love, increase of your peace and joy, increase in provision, increase in the other things which make us more closely conformed to the image of Jesus. There are more channels of provision available to you in ministry when you are in right relationships; therefore, there will be increase in everything.

We will increase corporately, as the members of this Body rightly relate to one another. We will grow numerically. We will increase financially. We will increase in our ability to impact our city and our community.

And the environment which encompasses all of this will be love. The love of God should be flowing. One thing I want people to say, more than anything else, when they come to our church for the first time is this: "Man, that place is filled with love!" That can only happen when we are rightly related to one another, when our relationships are established on a sound, scriptural basis and our communication is not distorted, but rather we speak the truth in love.

23

OUR DESENSITIZED CULTURE

A real impediment to communication in our world today is a tendency to commit falsehoods. Everyone engages to some degree or another in telling falsehoods. The reason why is that our culture has desensitized us to falsehood. However, the consequences of our disregard for truth are in evidence all around us. Think about it. Banks frequently will not cash checks for someone who is from out of town. Stores generally will not take returned merchandise without a sales receipt. Television monitors scan the aisles of stores looking for shoplifters. Everyone knows what a dead-bolt lock is. We have guard dogs, alarm systems, fences, lockers, chains, safes, lie detector tests and bloodhounds. Our entire society gives evidence to our accommodation of falsehood and dishonesty.

The curious thing, however, is that we are not nearly as concerned about the existence of that behavior as we are about protecting ourselves from its consequences. We accommodate a culture given over to a misrepresentation of truth. Because of that, we continue to desensitize ourselves to the problem that plagues us.

Falsehoods are raining down on our heads through the media every day. We are hypnotized with messages to buy this soap, that spray, this burial plot, that vacation—everything imaginable. We are told they are exaggerated claims, but we accept them as part of our culture.

It Gets Worse

Worse than that, we are sold a pile of falsehoods about who we are and what is going to make us happy in life. We accept the false notion about values we should hold dear to our hearts. Then when we really get unhappy, we don't know what to blame other than, "I don't have Calvin Klein jeans. That will make me happy." Or, "I don't have a new Ford Bronco." Or, "I don't have a new house." Or, "Wait. I think this will make me happy. No. That will make me happy." We are sold false notions of where happiness comes from, and we do not know how to deal with discontent when it comes.

We grow up in this environment, a culture desensitized to falsehood, and wonder why it is so easy for us to misrepresent the truth.

I read a study a few years ago which indicated that the average person tells about 200 lies a day.[1] That number also includes exaggerations, which are falsehoods we call white lies. Isn't that unreal—200 a day.

In our casual conversation, the tendency is to shade the truth for a variety of reasons. How many of us have called in sick this year just because we did not really want to go to work? After all, we have a couple of sick days left and we don't want to lose them. So we call in sick and go fishing.

The Acid Test

Have you ever fudged on your income tax a little bit? It is ironic to me that the IRS finds virtually all mistakes to their favor. They seldom refund more money than was claimed.

If you were a pastor, you would be amazed, as I am, at the opinions expressed by married couples who are in counseling and having difficulties. If you talk to the two partners separately, you get two totally different stories. These are Christian people who are supposed to put a high premium on the truth. But talk to them separately and you will get two totally different tales; the only way to get at the truth is to get the couple together.

Or maybe someone you have not seen in a long time calls you and you tell them, "Yes, come on over. I'd love to see you." Then you hang up the phone and say, "Man, I don't have time to do this. Why am I doing this? I have to clean the house. I don't want to see that person." Well, why did you tell him to come over?

Or you are in a meeting at work and you tell someone, "Yes, I'd love to do that for you." You leave the meeting and gripe about what you agreed to do because you really didn't want to do it. You were just trying to be nice.

Or you tell someone, "Whatever you want to do is fine with me." Then he does what he wants to do, and you get upset because it is not what you wanted him to do.

We are desensitized to falsehood. We do not like honest rejection, so we do things we dislike and then grumble about it. Conversely, we manipulate relationships in order to gain what we want by imposing a sense of guilt on someone else.

Hundreds of little things we do are nothing more than propagating falsehood. We wonder why our relationships hang by a thread when, in fact, we are more honest with our dogs and cats than we are with people.

Learn how to communicate truth, and do it in love. It will absolutely transform your relationships.

ADMIT IT, AND QUIT IT

First of all, we must confront the fact that we have a problem in this area. We have to acknowledge the need to focus our attention on the truth and make a deliberate effort to change before it will ever happen.

What is the truth? Truth takes two forms. There is spiritual truth, and there is empirical truth, which is based on observation and experiences.

There is truth that relates to the realm of the unseen; it is spiritual truth regarding issues we cannot confirm through natural reasoning or sensory perception. That spiritual truth originates in the Bible: God is a spirit and His Word is spirit as well. (John 6:63.) Therefore, to discover spiritual truth, God and His Word have to be the foundation for our search. Anything else you choose to believe has only one other source of origin—the very untrustworthy mind of man.

THE DEPENDABLE WORD

Your choice is pretty clear: either you choose to believe the Word of God, or you choose to believe someone's opinion. I choose the Word of God. It has come to us over thousands of years through the mouths of hundreds of prophets, and it presents a perfect picture of God's plan for man.

It is appropriate for us to engage in mathematics and science and rational thinking as it relates to this universe. God gave us our senses to perceive His creation so we could discern the truth of the natural realm. We are to use our brains for that purpose, not to try to disprove it. But be aware that you cannot use empirical truth to understand the truth which is spiritual. Spiritual truth will clarify and illuminate empirical truths for us, but empirical truth or natural reasoning will not illuminate things of the Spirit. Why not? Because, as it says in 1 Corinthians 2:14, **The natural man receiveth not the things of the Spirit of God: for they are foolishness unto him: neither can he know them, because they are spiritually discerned.**

Telling Yourself the Truth

You must be telling yourself the truth which originates with the Word of God. You must base your life on its truth so there are no wrong beliefs to encumber your communication with other people. And you have to be very honest about your motives, your fears, your insecurities and the things that you deal with in order for your communication to be truthful. You have to tell yourself the truth about your own heart and base that examination on the single source of truth, which is the Word of God.

> *You have to tell yourself the truth about your own heart and base that examination on the single source of truth, which is the Word of God.*

The integrity of your word is related to your ability to believe God will perform His Word. If you cannot trust yourself to tell the truth, how can you trust God to make His promises true? There is a link between integrity and faith.

Making It Personal

Many people wish they could believe the Word. The problem is they do not believe it applies to them personally. Lots of folks have said to me, "It's wonderful that the Bible promises healing. I want to believe that. But I haven't been able to internalize it for myself or come to that place of knowing." They have not come to that place of faith where it will produce a result.

There are others who have labored hard for years to rise above a level of poverty which has burdened them, but they are never quite able to do it. Somehow they cannot see beyond the stack of bills to believe that God is going to meet their need.

Very often and very probably that inability to come into a place of faith which will bring the answer is tied to the question of personal integrity.

"WE WRESTLE NOT..."

For we wrestle not against flesh and blood, but against principalities, against powers, against the rulers of the darkness of this world, against spiritual wickedness in high places. Wherefore take unto you the whole armour of God, that ye may be able to withstand in the evil day, and having done all, to stand.

Stand therefore, having your loins girt about with truth, and having on the breastplate of righteousness; And your feet shod with the preparation of the gospel of peace; Above all, taking the shield of faith, wherewith ye shall be able to quench all the fiery darts of the wicked.

And take the helmet of salvation, and the sword of the Spirit, which is the word of God.

Ephesians 6:12-18

God provides us with spiritual armor to enable us to stand against all the difficult times which come against us.

Peter said, **Beloved, think it not strange concerning the fiery trial which is to try you.** (1 Peter 4:12). And Jesus said in John 16:33, **In the world ye shall have tribulation.** Where are we living right now? In the world. But He went on to say, **Be of good cheer; I have overcome the world.**

The Devil is going to try to engage us in battle. It could be physically, financially, relationally; it could be many different ways. But the key to standing through the battle is the spiritual armor God gives us in Ephesians 6. We must have each piece of armor in place if we are going to be able to stand. They are all important, but the one I want to look at is in verse 14: **Stand therefore, having your loins girt about with truth, and having on** *the breastplate of righteousness.*

THE BREASTPLATE OF INTEGRITY

The Amplified Bible renders that the **breastplate of integrity.** Integrity is nothing more than honesty, speaking the truth and then acting upon the truth you have spoken. Notice, too, that the breastplate of integrity covers the most important part of your spiritual being—the heart. God said that out of the heart flow the issues of life. (Prov. 4:23.) How is that possible? Because the heart of man in Scripture is the place where faith is conceived and belief begins. The breastplate provides protection for your heart while faith is born.

So guard your heart. Wear the breastplate of integrity and tell the truth in love, thus protecting yourself from our desensitized culture.

24

THE WORD IN YOUR HEART

The sower soweth the word. And these are they by the way side, where the word is sown; but when they have heard, Satan cometh immediately, and taketh away the word that was sown in their hearts.

And these are they likewise which are sown on stony ground; who, when they have heard the word, immediately receive it with gladness; and have no root in themselves, and so endure but for a time: afterward, when affliction or persecution ariseth for the word's sake, immediately they are offended.

And these are they which are sown among thorns; such as hear the word, and the cares of this world, and the deceitfulness of riches, and the lusts of other things entering in, choke the word, and it becometh unfruitful.

And these are they which are sown on good ground; such as hear the word, and receive it, and bring forth fruit, some thirtyfold, some sixty, and some an hundred.

Mark 4:14-20

We want to be like the last example Jesus spoke of which is good ground. The word *ground* refers to the human heart, since that is where the Word is sown. We see that from what Jesus says in verse 15: **Satan cometh immediately, and taketh away the word that was sown *in their hearts*.**

So the ground referred to in this parable is analogous to the human heart. And we want to be the good ground that produces the fruit of the Word of God, some thirtyfold, some sixtyfold, some a hundredfold. It is a glorious promise to you and me that we can produce that kind of fruit.

CIRCUMSTANCES FROM HELL

Why didn't the other people who heard the Word produce fruit? Verse 15 begins, **These are they by the way side where the word is sown.** The Word of God was sown there. They heard that Jesus heals. They heard that He provides and that they did not have to live in lack and poverty anymore. But the reason that didn't produce fruit is found at the end of verse 15: **But when they have heard, Satan cometh immediately, and taketh away the word that was sown in their hearts.**

Satan comes with circumstance. The car breaks down; an unexpected bill comes in the mail. He comes with circumstance to steal the Word sown in your heart. And if he can do that, you have aborted the conception of faith that had taken place. Even when faith is conceived, if Satan can get to you, he will abort it and you will not produce fruit.

The breastplate of truth, or integrity, provides the spiritual covering for your heart that makes certain you will not be a "wayside" Christian. The breastplate also insures that the Devil will not be able to steal the seed of the Word before it has produced faith to receive.

WIMPED OUT

Mark 4:16 continues, **These are they likewise which are sown on stony ground.** This person hears the Word and gets excited about it. He rejoices in it until the hard times of affliction and persecution come. Someone calls him a Jesus freak or a fanatic, and because his heart was unprotected, he turns his back on the Word that was sown. The persecution and affliction went straight to his heart and aborted the Word that had been conceived there. What is his protection? It is the breastplate of integrity. It is the only piece of spiritual armor designed specifically to protect the heart.

Then look at the last guy. Verses 18 and 19 say,

> **And these are they which are sown among thorns; such as hear the word, and the cares of this world, and the deceitfulness of riches, and the lusts of other things entering in, choke the word, and it becometh unfruitful.**

This person actually produces fruit, but the cares of this world, the deceitfulness of riches and the lusts of other things enter in and choke the Word and it becomes unfruitful. Your protection against those Word-choking weeds growing in your heart is the breastplate of truth, or integrity.

Saint of God, for your own welfare, in your walk with God and in your relationships and your ministry, you must first of all become absolutely determined to develop a total truth habit. In other words, you develop the habit of speaking the truth in love. (Eph. 4:15.) No matter what the cost, no matter how it may seem to hurt, we have to tell the truth. It is the protection God has provided for our hearts.

THE LAST TWO WORDS

I said to speak the truth in love. Don't forget those last two words: *in love.* Speaking the truth alone can be a damaging thing. It can be a sharp sword that cuts and hurts and wounds. When the truth is wielded in that fashion, it does not bring what God wants to bring to a person's life.

There have been books written about winning by intimidating people and how to use that approach in personal relationships to generate the results you want. That is straight from the pit of hell and completely demonic in its origin. There is a lot of that influence in some secular teaching regarding communication skills. Stay away from that teaching. The Bible has too many good things to say about communication for you to resort to the Devil's tactics.

THE ESSENCE OF EFFECTIVE COMMUNICATION

The essence, or the heart and soul, of effective communication is truth. The Word points that out time and again. Ephesians 4:15 summarizes it. **But speaking the truth in love, may** [you] **grow up into him in all things, which is the head, even Christ.** Speak the truth in love, and then you can expect to grow up into Him in all things. Speaking the truth and doing so in love is effective communication.

If we are going to be leaders we have to mature in Christ. Paul says, **Henceforth be no more children** (Eph. 4:14). He is not talking about actual children; he is talking about spiritual children.

Being a leader means you have to grow up. You have to stop being children, **Tossed to and fro, and carried about with every wind of doctrine, by the sleight of men, and cunning craftiness, whereby they lie in wait to deceive** (v. 14). This is the world's way.

If we are going to grow up in Christ and be mature—not children conformed to the way of the world—then we must move away from the deception and manipulation that is so much a part of our lives. There is no room for hidden agendas; there is absolutely no room for deception or manipulation.

THE CORNERSTONE OF EFFECTIVE COMMUNICATION

Truth is the cornerstone of effective communication. We see this again in verse 25: **Wherefore putting away lying, speak every man truth with his neighbour.**

The way we conduct our relationships has to be characterized by integrity, loyalty, compassion and a genuine care for the people who work with us and for us. These are the ways we build the trust which will enable them to follow us.

HIDDEN AGENDAS

As you progress in leadership, at some point you will have to terminate someone's employment. On occasion, you will come across an employee who has demonstrated behavior that reflects a hidden agenda. They have their own best interests at heart, not the ministry's. They have not been faithful to pursue the vision of the ministry; they are in it for what they can get out of it.

This situation has to be dealt with quickly, because that spirit is infectious; it will be imparted to other people. If you have made an effort to point out that correction is needed, yet the person refuses to receive it, you will have to fire that person—and the sooner you do it the better.

Don't go on a witch-hunt, however. Distinguish between the shading of the truth, which is a normal fleshly tendency we all have to guard against, and intentional manipulation and deception.

As a leader, you must produce a non-threatening environment for the people who work for you in order to promote communication based on truth. That is why winning by intimidation does not work. The most productive work environment is one in which the employees feel completely unthreatened in terms of job security, self-esteem and self-image, as well as financial and material welfare.

YOUR OWN IMPORTANCE

The way you see yourself and feel about yourself is important to you. You need to feel good about yourself. That is why the Bible talks so much about who you are in Christ.

If you had a leader or manager who constantly criticized your performance or gave the impression he did not trust you out of his sight, that is a major threat to your self-esteem. And a threatening environment will corrupt communication and promote falsehood.

But when the Word is sown into the good ground of your heart, then you can begin to see yourself as God sees you—in Christ.

25

CREATING A NON-THREATENING
ENVIRONMENT

Imagine for a moment you are driving home at dusk. It is almost dark. You are on a lonely country road, and then your car breaks down. This big black car with windows tinted so dark you cannot see inside drives up beside you and slows to a stop. The window opens just a crack, and this voice says, "May I help you?"

The sense of a physical threat would probably cause you to lock your doors and say, "No, thank you!" even though it could have been a father, a brother or a friend in that car, hidden behind those dark windows.

Your perception of a threat to your physical well-being distorted the question, which was really very innocent, and it made you hear something which was not really there. The perceived threat caused you to refuse help when you truly needed it.

To promote effective communication, you must create a non-threatening environment. But how do you deal with conflict without creating a threatening environment? How do you confront poor performance or wrong behavior? If you are a leader, you have to be confrontational sometimes.

CREATING A NON-THREATENING ENVIRONMENT

I think many of us have a wrong understanding of what confrontation really is. To most of us, confrontation means to threaten. They think that when you confront, you threaten. That is incorrect. To confront means "to bring face to face."[1] You face error and deal with it. As a leader, you have to be confrontational in a way that does not produce a threatening environment or cause the other person to put up walls. So the greatest challenge in leadership communication is to deal successfully with the problems which have to be confronted and resolve conflict while still maintaining a non-threatening environment.

THE PERSECUTION COMPLEX

There are some people who will feel threatened no matter how carefully you follow the direction of Scripture. They feel like everybody is after them. They have a persecution complex. Maybe they grew up in a family where they were criticized from the moment they got up in the morning till they went to bed at night. Who knows why they do it, but they take everything you say the wrong way.

You can pray for that person, you can minister to them and you can encourage them to change in this area, but ultimately you need to realize as a leader that no matter how careful you are, these folks are always going to be a little on edge.

The measure of your success as a leader will never be governed by the fact that no one ever took offense at you. All you can do is have "clean hands and a pure heart," knowing you have done the best you can to provide an environment in which that is not going to occur. If it does, however, just make sure you do not take offense over their being offended!

But in the routine matter of resolving conflict and confronting wrong behavior in order to bring change to others' effort, there is a way to approach them so they are able to receive the correction without being unduly hurt or personally threatened. Let's see how Jesus did it.

JESUS, OUR EXAMPLE

As a leader, from time to time you are going to have to say hard things to the people who work for you. They may not want to hear those hard things. However, if they are going to grow in the Lord as well as produce the results organizationally that you desire, they will have to hear them. But you can look to Jesus as an example of how to do it.

In Revelation 2, Jesus dealt with seven churches, all of which needed correction. He had some hard things to say to them.

Jesus spoke to the church of Ephesus saying,

I know thy works, and thy labour, and thy patience, and how thou canst not bear them which are evil: and thou hast tried them which say they are apostles, and are not, and hast found them liars: And hast borne, and hast patience, and for my name's sake hast laboured, and hast not fainted. Nevertheless I have somewhat against thee.

Revelation 2:2-4

Then He outlined His grievances with the church of Ephesus.

Later He spoke to the church in Pergamos.

And to the angel of the church in Pergamos write; These things saith he which hath the sharp sword with two edges; I know thy works and where thou dwellest, even

where Satan's seat is: and thou holdest fast my name, and hast not denied my faith, even in those days wherein Antipas was my faithful martyr, who was slain among you, where Satan dwelleth. But I have a few things against thee.

Revelation 2:12-14

He spoke, also, to the church in Thyatira, saying,

I know thy works, and charity, and service, and faith, and thy patience, and thy works; and the last to be more than the first. Notwithstanding I have a few things against thee.

Revelation 2:19,20

THE PATTERN OF CORRECTION

Do you see His pattern of correction? He always acknowledged their value, their contribution and their good effort before He brought correction. He let them know they were important and acknowledged what they had done first.

When you bring correction to someone, if he is confident that you are aware of his positive contribution and the fact that his heart is right, then it is a lot easier for him to listen to what you have to say about correcting an aspect of his behavior or changing the direction of his activity.

THE WRONG WAY TO CONFRONT

This method of confrontation can be used wrongly as well. It is meaningless to go to someone and say, "I want you to know that I appreciate what you did the other day, but you have to straighten up here and do this." You cannot simply drop a compliment before you deliver a stinging criticism.

If you will consistently praise, reward employees with your gratitude and give recognition for things done well, when the day comes that you have to correct, you have laid the foundation to bring that correction with minimal threat to those corrected. They know you are aware of the right things they have done and the good moves they have made. They know you care.

If you are deliberate in laying that foundation, when you sit down with employees to offer correction, they are generally open to receive the things you have to say.

FIRST THINGS FIRST

When it is time to confront, the first thing you have to do is make sure your heart is right. People are different when it comes to confrontation. It has a lot to do with personality and upbringing. Some people can't wait to jump on someone. Some people are hesitant to confront about anything. You have to be aware of that weakness because it will cause you to let things slide that should not slide.

Do not be reluctant to confront. It may not be the most pleasant task of your day. It is never fun to criticize someone's performance, particularly if you like him or he is important to the organization. But it is a serious leadership weakness if you cannot constructively confront those you are responsible for. You are going to have to confront regularly in order to get the results you want. That's just a part of leadership.

The other side of the coin is the aggressive leader who finds some sort of self-gratification or reinforcement of his personal value by emphasizing the faults of another. Most of us have encountered people like this. If that happens to describe your approach to dealing with problems, then be aware that you have just as much a weakness as the person who does not like to confront.

KEEP THE GOAL IN MIND

The goal is to keep from producing a threatening environment if you can. However, when confrontation becomes necessary, remember, timing is very important. If there is a lot of distraction or other activity going on at that moment, put off your discussion, because distraction will dilute the effectiveness of your correction. You must have the person's attention, so be sensitive to the timing issue.

DON'T DUMP THE GUNNYSACK

When it is time to confront, be sure you have your emotions in check and are not doing it out of anger. Most of all, be sure you don't "dump the gunnysack." Stick to the issue at hand. Do not drag out all the complaints about this employee which you have been storing away for the last six months—all the things you haven't said anything about because they are really too small to have a special meeting over, but which, now that you have their attention, *you want to talk about!* Do not let it become that kind of meeting. Be singular in your purpose.

Remain focused. Before your meeting ask yourself why you are sitting down with them. If you had only two minutes with them, what would you want them to understand? Can you reduce the issue to one question and one problem-solving answer?

Then when you confront, follow Jesus' model, reinforcing their positive contributions and gifts and talents and reaffirming your concern for them.

NO FLOWERS, NO APOLOGIES

Simply state what the problem is. Send no flowers, and make no apologies. In other words, don't make excuses for having to speak with them. Just say something like, "Hey, look, you've been late to the last four staff meetings, and I want you to know that is not acceptable. Is there a reason I'm not aware of that is causing this to happen? If there is, I'd like you to tell me about it." Then listen and hear what they have to say.

If there is no acceptable reason for their behavior, you must let them know it needs to be changed. Make sure they understand why their behavior is a problem and why it must be changed.

Your goal is to help them understand your reason for saying this is unacceptable behavior. You have the positional authority. You could say, "This is unacceptable. Change it." But that is contrary to your best interests as well as theirs.

> *You will have better results if they understand why it is not acceptable performance. Help them to reason it out.*

You will have better results if they understand why it is not acceptable performance. Help them to reason it out. But, remember, you must be as willing to listen as you expect them to be. If you cannot come to an agreement, maybe the problem is yours, not theirs.

ONE...TWO...THREE

You should not have any problem saying, "This has to change because...," and list your reasons—one, two, three. If they have any common sense, they will say, "Yes, I see that." Remember, your goal is to get them to change direction, to see the wisdom in what you are saying and agree to make the necessary changes.

Be aware that you are doing this after having reinforced their value to you and to the organization. So hopefully they are not threatened by your discussion and they can respond without offense. Then they can look logically at your reasoning and say, "Yes, I agree with that." And then you have the basis for change.

FORGET ABOUT IT!

Once they change their behavior, do not bring it up again. A lot of leaders keep a log of the things their people do wrong so they can remind them every now and then when they get out of line.

God says that when we make a mistake, He forgets about it. He puts it as far from Him as the East is from the West and remembers it no more. (Ps. 103:12.) He is your example. That means that once you have dealt with an issue, forget about it.

When you do not forget about it, even though the person has changed his behavior in that area, emotionally you are piling up negatives which give you an unrealistic, inappropriate and unscriptural view of the person and his place in your organization.

When you do forget about it, you reinforce in his mind his value to you and your integrity as a leader. And all that must remain intact if he is going to continue following you.

So much rides on our being able to confront successfully and effectively while creating a non-threatening environment. Those being confronted must come away from the discussion knowing that one deficient area does not negate the good they have done so far. That was Jesus' way, and we must learn to make it our way.

26

CONFLICT RESOLUTION

Confrontation is not the same as conflict. Confrontation results when behavioral changes are necessary. Conflict results when someone disagrees with the direction you bring. A lot of people are slow to confront because of the potential for conflict. But conflict does not occur until someone resists the change you want to see him make.

Understand that our warfare is not against flesh and blood, but against principalities and powers, rulers of darkness and spiritual wickedness in high places. (Eph. 6:12.) Our warfare is spiritual.

For a long time, this was a difficult area for me in my Christianity. It didn't take much faith for me to believe in God. All you had to do was look at the intricacies of creation, and if you have an IQ of more than ten, you could figure out that there is a God. But I had a problem with the Devil.

OUR ARCH ENEMY, THE DEVIL

I associated the Devil, or this entity the Bible calls Satan, as a generalization for evil and not really as a personality or someone I had to contend with. I saw him as a ghost or goblin associated with Halloween—more of a comical figure, but certainly not real. So for a lot of years, I wondered why things would "go sideways" sometimes. The answer, very simply, is that if you do not know there is an enemy, you cannot defend yourself against him.

There is a very real evil entity called Satan. You do not have to run from him, but you do have to know he is there. However, you do not have to get uptight about him; you have the blood of Jesus and the name of Jesus, and according to the Word of God, Satan is already a defeated foe. That's what Calvary was all about.

Satan and his demonic host have been stripped of all power. The only way he can work his purpose in your life and thwart the will of God is through deception.

DIVIDE AND CONQUER

Now, this has everything to do with our subject of conflict resolution, because one of Satan's primary efforts in any corporate body of believers is to divide. He has very few other strategies he can employ against a group of believers other than to bring division. Why division? Because **If a house be divided against itself, that house cannot stand.** (Mark 3:25).

If you have anyone under your authority, anyone over whom you exercise godly influence, then you can rest assured the Enemy is going to make an effort to produce schism in that group. Jesus gave us some principles for dealing with this.

I am the good shepherd: the good shepherd giveth his life for the sheep. But he that is an hireling, and not the

shepherd, whose own the sheep are not, seeth the wolf coming, and leaveth the sheep, and fleeth: and the wolf catcheth them, and scattereth the sheep.

John 10:11,12

Jesus is the Chief Shepherd, and pastors are under-shepherds. The wolf in Scripture is an analogy for the one who divides.

As a leader, you have a primary charge to be aware of the wolf and to prevent his scattering the flock for which you are responsible.

The wolf will come—someone operating by a wrong spirit, making waves, being contentious, producing strife and division in a Body of believers or a group of people, sometimes without even being aware of it.

A HIRELING IN THE PULPIT

Jesus said if the person who is leading the flock is not a shepherd but instead is a hireling, one the Lord has not given the authority to stand in that office, then when the wolf of division comes, there is no anointing to drive him away.

I have seen occasions when a pastoral search committee will find someone and hire him to head up a church because he has three doc-torates and a lot of initials behind his name. It seems like he should be the right one. But if he is not the one God has called—and no amount of natural education can earn the call of God—there will be no anoint-ing to drive away the wolf of division.

DISCERNING THE WOLF IN THE FLOCK

We see more about the wolf in Matthew 7:15: **Beware of false prophets, which come to you in sheep's clothing, but inwardly they are ravening wolves.** A wolf, a person being influenced by the wrong spirit to produce division, doesn't necessarily look like a wolf.

If a wolf knocked on your door, you wouldn't let him in because you know he is a wolf; you would chase him out the back. Forget it. Wolves never look like wolves. I hear people say, "Well, they were so nice and so sweet." That's the way they look. They come in sheep's clothing, but inwardly they are ravening wolves.

Scripture goes on to say in verse 16, **Ye shall know them by their fruits.** We read later, in verses 21 and 22,

> **Not every one that saith unto me, Lord, Lord, shall enter into the kingdom of heaven; but he that doeth the will of my Father which is in heaven.**
>
> **Many will say to me in that day, Lord, Lord, have we not prophesied in thy name? and in thy name have cast out devils? and in thy name done many wonderful works?**

But that's not how you judge the validity of ministry. The works they do are not the standards by which you judge their fruit. There are going to be occasions when someone standing in an office of ministry produces division in the body of Christ.

What is the wolf's fruit? Division. And there is no doubt that those efforts are going to be made by the enemy. Look at Acts 20:28-30:

> **Take heed therefore unto yourselves, and to all the flock, over the which the Holy Ghost hath made you over-seers, to feed the church of God, which he hath purchased with his own blood. For I know this, that after my depart-ing shall grievous wolves enter in among you, not sparing the flock. Also of your own selves shall men arise, speaking perverse things, to draw away disciples after them.**

SOURCES OF DIVISIVE INFLUENCE

There are two sources of divisive influence—external and internal. As Scripture says, **I know this, that after my departing shall griev-ous wolves enter in among you** (v. 29). Wolves will come from without and enter into a corporate Body of believers or a company of believers. Division takes a lot of different shapes.

A traveling ministry should reinforce and undergird what the pastor is doing in the local church and help produce growth in a cohesive effort toward the vision that God has given the pastor. That's one of the basic responsibilities of a traveling ministry. But I can remember a time ten or fifteen years ago when a traveling minister declared himself to be a prophet and made a circuit through about thirty local churches of many different denominations. Everywhere he went, there was division and contention.

The message was so deceptive that many of the pastors did not recognize the need to bring correction. The next thing you know, the pastor was hearing certain members of his congregation say, "We want you to do this or that. We want to know why you do not minister the way that prophet did. Why aren't those same signs and wonders happening in our church on a regular basis?" And bang, bang, bang—about a dozen churches split in no time at all. That tells you very quickly that the "prophet" was a wolf. Jesus said you would know them by their fruit.

This particular man emphasized the miraculous and the prophetic. "Lord, Lord, didn't I say many wonderful things in Thy name?" Jesus warned these wolves would say this. (Matt. 7:22.) But, no, that's not the fruit you measure by. You know they are wolves if there is a divisive influence.

DIVISION ARISING FROM THE BODY

The passage we just read in Acts tells us of another way for the wolf to enter in: **Also of your own selves shall men arise, speaking perverse things.** In other words, occasionally someone in your Body of believers may begin acting by the wrong spirit—usually unknowingly—and they will raise up a banner to attract people to themselves.

I can remember early in our ministry when there was a real neat church member who was an evangelist. He had a heart for Haiti. The only problem was, I didn't. Haiti was not a part of our vision for missions at that point in time.

Now, that did not mean he was wrong. It just meant he was in the wrong place. But I did not realize that right away. One Sunday I learned that about a dozen of our church members were going to go with him on a missions trip to Haiti. Suddenly I saw what was happening.

That sounds okay, doesn't it? This man had a heart for Haiti, he was doing some good things and he was generating a following who would fund his missions thrust to Haiti.

RIGHT HEART, WRONG HEAD

What happened was that the Enemy raised up a man who operated by the wrong spirit, even though he loved the Lord. He was deceived. He thought it was perfectly all right to announce his intentions to take a group to Haiti, but he drew a large number of the people—people called to support the vision of the church—off to this other project in Haiti. He garnered their support both financially and prayerfully, as well as their investment of time and effort. He didn't understand these principles, so he was having a divisive influence in the ministry.

Finally, I had to tell him that there was another church somewhere else that would support him in his work in Haiti and it wasn't ours. His heart was right; his head was wrong. He did find another church that shared his vision, and he plugged in with them. But in our church he had a divisive influence.

I had another guy in the music ministry who came to me and said, "I want to start an outreach band to go downtown."

I said, "No, brother, I appreciate that, but right now all of our resources for our music ministry are invested in something else, and we're not able to do that." The next thing I knew, he was out in the congregation rounding up musicians on his own, preparing to take an outreach band downtown.

"Hey, what's wrong with that? This guy just wants to reach the lost," I can hear people say. I will tell you what is wrong with it: it produced division in the body of Christ. He was doing exactly what Acts 20:30 refers to: **Also of your own selves shall men arise, speaking perverse things, to draw away disciples after them.** These men were drawing disciples away from the church where it pleased God to place them, and it was drawing them away from the vision they were to support and be a part of.

> *I do not think most people who are used in a way that produces contention and division in a local body really know what they are doing.*

RECOGNIZING DIVISION

As a leader, you have to recognize this or you will never have an organization that experiences any long-term success, either in the secular world or in ministry. As far as being a leader is concerned, one of your challenges is going to be not letting that devil of schism and division touch your organization, your ministry, your church or your business, because it is the primary way the Enemy will keep you from realizing the full potential you have otherwise.

THEY KNOW NOT WHAT THEY DO

I do not think most people who are used in a way that produces contention and division in a local body really know what they are doing. I do not think most of them are aware of it. They are simply young Christians, in many cases, ignorant of the Scripture. Many times they are zealous and want to do something for God, and in their zeal, they overstep their boundaries or do not do it the way God says.

So as a leader, when these situations present themselves, you have an opportunity to exercise your communication skills. Isn't that exciting? You have another chance to become skilled as a communicator in resolving conflict.

As a leader, because you have the title and the position, you pursue conflict resolution by declaring your right to remind them of God's order of authority, your place in that order of authority over them and of their need to submit to that order so they are not in rebellion to the Holy Spirit. But if that is your approach to conflict resolution, you will never get off the second, or positional, level of leadership. People will follow you only because they have to.

TIMING, TIMING, TIMING

Conflict resolution cannot occur when emotions are in an upheaval or when anger is present. And if that is the case when you are trying to deal with the conflict, do not go any further. Set it aside and come back to it later. If emotions are running high and there have been hard words, you may regret it if you pursue it further.

Very logically your approach to the matter has to be this. No matter what the conflict is, the Bible says in Amos 3:3 that two cannot walk together except they be agreed. You cannot allow conflict to go unresolved.

So when you sit down with them, say, "I'm sorry you are not in agreement with the direction I feel is appropriate. I do not want to impose this on you. I want your agreement because the Bible says that two cannot walk together except they be agreed. So let's talk about this, and if there is a deeper root to your disagreement, I'd like to hear about it. My goal as the person you are accountable to is that there be no unresolved conflict or problems between us."

Then get them talking, and remember the number one rule of good communication: You listen.

VENTING

Most of the time, no matter how serious the conflict may seem, resolution is found simply in the other person's ability to vent a little bit. Usually after they have vented, they feel kind of silly, but by then it is on the table, they have said what they needed to and things can settle down. Most of the time, conflict is a result of unspoken feelings or frustrations or resentments. Therefore, most of the time just having the opportunity to get it out is enough to resolve the issue.

If they are familiar with the Word of God, they cannot argue with you when you say, "We're going to get into agreement. We cannot let this go on unresolved." Their desire to resolve the conflict will most probably be as strong as yours.

27

LEADERSHIP AND SUBMISSION

The world's way of handling conflict is not the Kingdom's way. Oftentimes labor has a totally different point of view from management, and the only way to resolve the differences is through a walkout, or a strike—some means of forcing the other side to give in. For the body of Christ, the Scripture is clear. We must walk together in one accord and harmony.

In a marriage, for example, the husband can say, "The Bible says I'm the head; therefore, you do what I say. Submit, woman." If you have ever done that, you know what a mistake it is. It does not work.

You must have heard about the guy who went to a submission seminar to learn how to be the spiritual head of his house. He came back after three days at the seminar and told his wife, "I've got this thing down now, honey. I'm the head of this house. I'm going to take my place; you submit, woman."

He didn't see her for two or three days. But by then he was able to open one eye just a little bit. Like I said, it doesn't work.

VOLUNTARY SUBMISSION

Submission, if it is to work, has to be voluntary. No matter what level of authority we are talking about, it can never be forced. Forced submission produces either bondage and servitude or rebellion. So as a leader in the body of Christ, it is your task in conflict resolution to gain willful submission to the direction you bring, and you should approach it just as you would a marriage relationship.

What do we teach in marriage? We teach that a husband and wife can always bring themselves to a place of agreement. The husband should never exercise his position of authority as head of the wife without regard for her opinion or concerns. She was given to him because he needs her. Without her, they are both incomplete. Together, they are an unbeatable team. He is not going to inherit the grace of this life by himself, because that is the way God has set it up.

That principle is true on any level of organizational authority. It is together, as a cooperative part of the body of Christ, that we are going to succeed. No individual is going to do it on his own.

THE GOAL — AGREEMENT

Your goal must be agreement, and on the points where there is conflict, sit down and lay out your rationale. Now it is true to say that one of the reasons God has set the levels of authority in the body of Christ is that someone has to make the final decision when there is no consensus.

Perhaps time constraints make it necessary to reach a decision without much discussion. On those occasions, you may have to say, "I really want your understanding in this matter. We have to move on, and we must do so in one accord and in harmony. That is what I expect from you even though my decision is not consistent with your opinion. Therefore, I can only expect you to support the decisions I make with your prayers and with your best effort."

A MATTER OF STYLE

Sometimes conflict arises because different people do things differently. In other words, it is not a matter of right or wrong—it is simply a matter of style. When you focus on the differences, there is always the potential for conflict, and often the problems raised will have nothing to do with the question at hand. Make sure to focus and build the relationship on the things you can agree upon, and if necessary, change the way you do something without changing your goals.

Sometimes when I get excited about something, I can seem a little heavy-handed in implementing it. In my enthusiasm, I might act prematurely, without considering the different people or situations which might be affected, and I generate a little stir. That is easily solved by my saying, "No problem. I can change the way I'm doing that. Sorry."

Some conflicts will not be resolved by that process and, unfortunately, the body of Christ is the worst example of that. When you look at the strife and division which has split churches over the decades, you realize how true that is. Some people are more interested in holding their offense even when they see it's the work of God that suffers. When a church splits, not only does it bring reproach to the name of God, it makes the body of Christ a laughingstock to the secular community: "Those Lutherans [or Baptists or charismatics] are at it again, fighting among themselves." I am convinced ninety-seven percent of all differences can be resolved.

It is only when you have gone through this process to resolve the conflict and you have no other recourse that you must consider asking someone to leave. Even if it is a person in your church, on your staff or in your business organization, if you cannot bring resolution through this process, you are going to have to say, "Adios."

If, however, you will go through this process, ninety-seven percent of the interpersonal conflict and the upheaval it causes within organizations will be resolved, and you will be on the road to success and blessing.

LOVE PEOPLE, NOT OPINIONS

What will really help you in dealing with conflict is your commitment to love people more than you love your own opinion. When you would rather protect your opinions than let go of them to benefit or bless another person, you can count on problems from those you are trying to lead. Be willing to yield to reason. Don't be dogmatic.

Thomas Jefferson made the statement that when it comes to matters of principle, defend it "to the t," but when it comes to the matters of preference, flow with the stream. I consider that very good advice. Opinions can produce unnecessary conflict. Love people more than your opinions.

MERCY MOTIVATED

When it comes to conflict resolution, give others the benefit of the doubt. If you do not have hard evidence about a situation, do not be suspicious, thinking the worst of someone. That is the world's way. God says we're to be merciful, and that means we're to give others the benefit of the doubt.

Learn to be flexible. Someone can have a better idea than you do. If that is the case, don't be so rigid in your approach to organization or ministry that you cannot change. We are creatures of habit. We tend to fall into patterns of behavior we are comfortable with. When someone comes up with a better idea than yours—which will happen frequently because there is wisdom in a multitude of counselors (Prov. 11:14)—go with the flow. It will be what is best for the organization.

A WAY OF ESCAPE

The Bible says we are to die to self, but the truth is, God created us with an ego. Sometimes we can abuse that and become self-centered in our activities, because our self-identity is important to us. If you back someone into a corner when you have to confront him and do not give him a way to save face, you have destroyed any possibility of working with that person again. Always provide a way of escape for those you must confront.

I have watched leaders do this. Someone may have done something legitimately wrong, and the one in charge just hammers him to pieces for it, giving him no way to save face. That leader has just made him a useless employee, because that person will never again submit to his leadership. I am not saying you should minimize the wrong the employee has done; however, he must have a way to leave that unpleasant moment with his self-esteem still intact. Besides, regardless of what he has done wrong, confrontation must always be about behavior, never about the person's worth as an individual.

FIRE STARTER OR FIREFIGHTER

Check your own attitude. When it comes to conflict resolution, do you have many conflicts going on lately? Is this getting to be the rule rather than the exception?

Some managers never have any conflict. Other managers always have a fire burning somewhere. If you always have conflict going on, there is a pretty good possibility the problem is with you. You will have to do some serious self-examination, because conflict should be the exception rather than the rule.

Don't overreact. Don't drop a bomb when a BB will do it. I know the heat of the moment always makes the issue seem more significant than it is. But that is why the Bible says in James 1:19 to be swift to hear, slow to speak and slow to anger. There may even be some instances when you should not respond at all. There may be a little ripple on the pond, but you will magnify it by giving it attention. Know when you have to respond, and do not overreact when you do.

View the conflict as an opportunity to learn, and it will help you avoid the tendency we all have, which is to avoid conflict. Use it to sharpen your skills as a communicator, to improve someone's performance in the Kingdom of God and to move the organization ahead.

TAKING THE RISK

Lastly, when it comes to conflict resolution, always be a risk taker. Risk rejection. Risk being wrong. Risk the unpleasant words that might come. Risk someone's anger. Risk being the one to step out and resolve the conflict. Don't ever let fear cause you to stand back and let conflict go unresolved. That will always do more harm than good.

Furthermore, if this is your style of leadership, you should have little trouble with submission.

28

NEGOTIATION

Now I beseech you, brethren, by the name of our Lord Jesus Christ, that ye all speak the same thing, and that there be no divisions among you; but that ye be perfectly joined together in the same mind and in the same judgment.

1 Corinthians 1:10

Paul is talking about walking together with others in agreement. *Agreement* means "harmony in opinion or feeling."[1] How do you get to a place of agreement if there are differences of opinion? You must negotiate. Now that is not a word that appears in either the Old or the New Testament, but it is a principle which permeates the Word of God. We are going to have to negotiate with others to resolve our differences; only then can we walk together in harmony.

We tend to say, "There are too many personality differences, too many differences of opinions. We cannot be perfectly joined together in the same mind, and the same judgment and of the same speech. That is an impossibility!"

Well, this is the challenge of leadership. We have to bring those entrusted to us by God to this place. When we do, we will see the other myriad problems begin to dissolve, because most of the challenges we have as leaders in the body of Christ are really offshoots of this one underlying consideration.

If you do not become skilled in the art of negotiation, you will never be successful at bringing your church into this place of same mind, same judgment, perfectly joined together. And you will not see the increase you want.

COMPROMISE

Negotiation is the resolution of differences in a way which is acceptable to both parties. Settlements normally fall into the category of either a compromise or a trade-off.

Compromise means "reaching a settlement by each side giving up part of its demands."[2] Neither side gets one-hundred percent of what it wants. Maybe you will get sixty percent of what you wanted and they will get sixty percent of what they wanted. But each side must approach the negotiation with this attitude: it is worth not getting everything you asked for in order to salvage the relationship.

A *trade-off* is "an exchange," meaning there may be a point of particular importance to one side which is not important to the other, so it is given up to them.[3] On the other side of the ledger there is something not quite as important to them, but which means more to you, so they give in on that point. That is a trade-off.

To become a skilled negotiator, you are going to have to confront the other person with the need to deal with the perceived conflict. You are going to have to convince him of your desire to resolve the differences.

Nobody likes the idea of negative emotions or perhaps even rejection. That is why so many people never confront differences. It can be distasteful. But your skill as a communicator, your ability to resolve conflict and, therefore, your ability to influence people hinges on your willingness to confront. You are going to have to initiate the process by confronting the people involved.

Let them know your motive for confronting them is not to humiliate them; neither is it to simply win the point. Your motive is to resolve the conflict in a way that is mutually beneficial to both parties. As a part of the confrontation, you have to communicate that up front, before they back away and close you off.

ESTABLISH YOUR REFUSAL PARAMETERS

There are some things God has told you to do which you are not going to be able to do differently. Period. So during that part of the negotiation there is no compromise. Establish your refusal parameters in your own mind before you go into the negotiation session.

Make a decision on all the things you are willing to trade off or compromise. Decide what points of the problem or difference you can yield on. Decide what you are willing to give up completely. That is your negotiating material right there.

Give all you can to the other person, employing the love of God. The Bible says love never fails. (1 Cor. 13:8.) Yield to his concerns everywhere you can without violating your refusal parameters or the Scripture.

AGREE TO RESOLVE

Do what you can to defuse the threat of confrontation by agreeing, first of all, that the conflict has to be resolved. Sit down with the other person and say, "Look, I know it may seem like our differences are insurmountable, but they're not. Otherwise, God wouldn't have told us to be of a same mind and same judgment. God will not tell us to do something we cannot do. And if He said He wants us to be of the same mind and same judgment because it is the only way either of us is going to experience His will and His blessing, then I want us to agree, brother, that we have to resolve this difference.

"If we will both make that determination, I am willing to yield to reason. I care about your concerns and your viewpoints. I assume the same is true for you."

IDENTIFY THE PRINCIPLE POINT OF DIFFERENCE

In many instances, particularly when a disagreement is several months or perhaps even years old, we do not really know what started it all. All we know is someone acted ugly. "He offended me. He lied. He did not treat me right. I just have a real problem with him." Most of the time, the communication has been distorted. Maybe one or two comments were taken out of context. Many times there is no solid basis for the conflict at all.

The first step in negotiating skillfully is to clearly identify and agree on the problem. In order to do this you must listen.

HEAR ACCURATELY

Communication involves the exchange of information or ideas, with an emphasis on *exchange* that very clearly eliminates those occasions on which you have given someone a piece of your mind. No communication occurred until there was a response, and then you measured the response to determine whether or not your communication was properly received.

Effective communication requires you to shape a message, deliver it and then wait for the response to see if the other person accurately received what you said. If he did not, then you have to adjust.

Most communication failures do not occur because someone did not go to college or he does not have a large vocabulary or excellent verbal skills. Most communication failures occur because of interference in the interpersonal environment, which comes from human emotion and social background. More than anything else, these are the two factors which distort the messages transmitted.

The interpersonal environment is filled with static, if you will, which inhibits or corrupts the communication before it reaches the ears of the receiver. Interpersonal static means things like different viewpoints: our upbringing, our background and racial or cultural considerations.

THE SQUELCH KNOB

When you communicate on an airplane radio, you have what is called a squelch knob. You turn up that squelch knob to match the sensitivity of your receiver so you can use the maximum range of your radio. But if you turn it too far, it can pick up static and outside interference, and then the message is completely distorted.

The same is true on the interpersonal level. In our environment there is a lot of extraneous "interpersonal noise" which can distort the idea you are trying to communicate. Such things as attitudes, prejudices, different points of view, family backgrounds and personal experiences are all things which will "encode" your message in a way which distorts the meaning of what you say.

To complicate matters, the person listening to you is dealing with his own interpersonal noise and twisting the squelch knob in an effort to filter out the static and understand what you have said.

If you are not aware of this, you will never be able to communicate effectively with other people. If you just spit out whatever is on your mind and give no thought to the things which can potentially distort your message, your listener may misunderstand, misinterpret your heart and give you an erroneous response.

To defeat the static in the interpersonal environment, be aware of its presence. Most people believe that just about everyone thinks the same way they do and will automatically understand what they say. That is a very naïve and wrong assumption. So how do we make adjustments?

Making adjustments is fine tuning in the art of negotiation—a subject we need to discuss in greater detail.

29

MAKING ADJUSTMENTS

Whether you are delivering a message from a pulpit or across a conference table, you will have to make adjustments for whatever potential interpersonal static may be in the environment. Some static is obvious. Depending on the people involved, you probably know what kinds of things will distort the message you send.

As you prepare what you want to say, as much as you can you should keep the other person's perspective in mind. It will shape how you present your case, not because you are trying to shade or alter the truth, but because you want him to accurately perceive what you say.

Do you remember what Jesus said in the parable of the sower? The first reason the Enemy is able to steal the seed of the Word is that the hearer does not understand what he has heard. If you cannot gain enough insight into someone's perspective to shape the message appropriately, it cannot take root. The Enemy will be able to come and steal it immediately.

In order to squelch the personal static successfully, you have to consider the emotional content of the conversation. If anger is present, you are going to have to defuse it, because when anger is present, communication is always distorted.

HEARING THE OTHER PERSON

The Lord says in James 1:19, **Be swift to hear, slow to speak.** The word hear in the Greek literally translated means "to understand."[1] It is not enough simply to hear the sounds another makes; it is a requirement to understand the other person's perspective.

Listen actively; don't sit there thinking of your response when you should be listening. The sad truth of our flesh is that we are usually too busy thinking of our response to listen accurately to everything the other person is saying. Most of us hear the first few sentences another person speaks, and then we immediately start thinking about how we are going to respond to what was said. We miss three-quarters of the message, and we wonder why there was so much misunderstanding in the conversation.

THE PARAPHRASE

To be certain you are hearing someone accurately, especially in conflict resolution, use paraphrases to reiterate to the person what you believe you have heard him say: "Okay. Let me be sure I've heard you right. I understand that you think I believe this and this and I did that. Is that what you said?"

This technique will keep both of you from misunderstanding. It also allows the other person an opportunity to validate your understanding, and it short-circuits distorted communication caused by the hurt feeling so often present in these kinds of exchanges.

Paraphrasing what the other person has said is one of the most effective tools I have ever used in becoming a good listener. It makes you listen to the other person. It enables that person to validate your interpretation, and it promotes valuable exchanges, making growth the result. The best communicator is a good listener. The Lord makes it clear: Be swift to hear.

Then He says to be slow to speak. That means do not engage your tongue before you engage your brain. Our responses are usually generated out of our emotions; we respond quickly to what has been said before we have intellectually measured the wisdom of saying what has popped into our minds.

If you establish a pattern of responding slowly, when you get to the point where you're ready to "flame someone," you can get hold of yourself. Take three or four breaths before you respond, particularly to something inflammatory. Be sure you hear what is really on the other person's mind before you answer.

UNDERSTAND YOUR FEELINGS

If you feel threatened, what you hear from someone will be distorted. You will not hear what he is saying because you are too busy constructing your defense and preparing your self-justification. Paraphrasing gives you time to cool off before you respond out of your hurt or anger, saying something you might later regret.

Then, when you are responding with your view of the problem, stay impersonal so the other person does not take it as an attack on his character.

Once the problem has been identified, you may uncover behavior on your part which has contributed to the point of difference. You may have said something or done something which gave an incorrect impression. If you are even partially at fault, admit it immediately. Assure the person you will change your behavior in that area, but remember your refusal parameters. Many times you can modify a behavior without compromising what God has called you to do.

INTENSITY AND ANGER

If you are an intense person by nature, sometimes your intensity can be misinterpreted as anger. At one time we received a lot of mail from our television audience. Many said I appeared hard and angry. The effect was that they could not hear the things God might say to them through me. So I had to make some behavior modification. I wasn't angry, but I learned to smile more and be more congenial. I did not have to change the message, nor did I have to change what God had called me to do. However, I did have to modify my behavior. One of the letters said, "I wish you'd smile more." So I started smiling more.

If your attitude says, "Hey, I'm the man. Take it or leave it," people are going to leave it.

ACCOUNTABILITY

The last adjustment in the negotiating process is to reach a settlement, one which is mutually satisfactory. But make sure it is a wise settlement. By that I mean, do not leave any ambiguity in what the settlement entails. Make sure both parties to the settlement understand clearly what the new responsibilities are, and make sure there is a standard of accountability which will help everyone adhere to his or her responsibilities.

It might be wise, if the conflict is significant enough, to put a written settlement in contract form. I do not mean to get legalistic about it. Most of the negotiating you do will not require anything this involved because it is on a surface level. But if you are resolving a serious conflict, written settlement terms might be wise.

I did it with my children as they were growing up. I'd say, "Here is the deal: you do this, and I do that. You do that, and I do this." Then we would write it down. The next time they forgot, I could show them what the agreement was, not as an excuse to criticize but as a means of putting them back on the right track. The agreement clearly stated the responsibilities of both parties, and it provided a standard of accountability.

A Third Party

The other alternative to a written settlement is to have a disinterested third party present—not as a mediator, but as a witness. This person should be someone respected by both parties of the conflict, who will provide a standard of accountability and may, on occasion, remind the people involved of what had been agreed.

Any settlement, whether written or verbal, must be definitive enough to make both parties accountable for what they have agreed to. It is good to say, "Well, just to be sure we do not forget what we have accomplished here, let me send you a memo or a letter which defines what we have agreed to do and how we have agreed to resolve the matter."

If someone objects and says writing it down makes him feel like you do not trust him, let him know it is not a matter of trust, but, rather, remind him that memories often play tricks on us over time.

The Wrong Church

It is conceivable that the other person is just in the wrong organization or wrong church. It is possible that for him to exercise what he has in his heart would bring division because leadership is going in a different direction. But somewhere there is a church which carries a vision where he can pursue his heart's desire without violating what God has directed him to do.

If that possibility becomes a reality, then tell him, "Friend, you are in the wrong place. This church is not the best place for you. I will pray and agree with you that you'll find the right place. I'll even help you in that process if I can. But, please do not do or say anything to promote a wider schism in this church while you are looking for a new one."

Make sure he knows the church is your responsibility and, should he return before attempting to reconcile the differences, he will be removed.

There is also the possibility you will encounter a person who is not in agreement with resolving the conflict. He is determined to promote his viewpoint regardless of any other biblical consideration. His heart is not right. He is being used of the Enemy to promote division. In that event, the Bible says, **Now I beseech you, brethren, mark them which cause divisions and offences contrary to the doctrine which ye have learned; and avoid them** (Rom. 16:17).

TAKE NOTE OF

I do not believe this is a public marking—making someone stand up to embarrass him. I believe it simply means take note of him for your own benefit. Mark him as someone causing division, someone you will not be involved with further.

If you have made every effort to reconcile—you have gone through the negotiating process, you have given everything love can give without violating your refusal parameters or what God has told you to do—and that person is still contentious and causing division, then mark him indeed.

The Scripture in Romans says to mark him and avoid him. And as a leader, you will have to instruct your church to avoid him. How do you do that? You say, "I have made my best effort to come to a successful resolution of the matter; my heart is clear in it, but I have had to ask this person to leave. He is an undesirable element in our congregation, and his heart is not right. The Bible tells me what I have to do. If he comes back without reconciliation, he will be removed."

If you think you might need to physically remove someone, a security person should help. I am not suggesting you jump on the erring person and haul him out the back door. But be firm; you must make your decision stick.

If the person has infected other members, go to them personally and say, "This is what is happening. We have asked him to leave, and we believe you are going to have to make a choice as well—follow him, or continue with us." It is important they understand that even if the one they are following has heard from God, if they go about it in a wrong spirit, they are in error. (James 3:13-18.)

Yes, I know this will take time and effort, but let it motivate you to become an even better listener. I also know it seems very hard, but, remember, if you make the adjustments to communicate well in the beginning, there will be fewer situations like this to handle in the long run.

30

NO OFFENSE TAKEN

If you are slow to respond when confronted, you have the opportunity to control that devilish threat that tries to rise up in your flesh—to take offense. Proverbs 16:24 makes the point: **Pleasant words are as an honeycomb, sweet to the soul, and health to the bones.**

Here is the Holy Spirit formula for how to produce a non-threatening environment for effective communication. First, listen. Respond slowly and deliberately, so you can make your response pleasant.

What are you doing? You are preserving the non-threatening environment. Those pleasant words will be sweet to the other person's soul, the emotional part of his being, which has the capacity to feel anger or hurt. When you speak pleasant words, you minister to his soul.

James 1:19 says to be **slow to wrath**. You have to keep anger out of the communication. Anger has only one place for expression in the life of the believer—toward the enemy of your soul, the Devil. The only appropriate anger is righteous indignation. Anger is never to be directed at people.

Ephesians 6:12 says we wrestle not against flesh and blood, but against principalities, powers, rulers of darkness and spiritual wickedness in high places. If anger becomes a part of your communication style as a leader, you are doomed, because it will immediately produce the threatening environment you are laboring to avoid.

BUT, WHAT IF...?

Well, you might ask, what if my employee is angry? What if he is wrathful? Proverbs 15:1 says, **A soft answer turneth away wrath.** So when you are communicating with one of your employees or someone you are responsible to direct, keep this in mind. Then meaningful direction can be imparted.

First, listen. (Yes, I know I just covered this. Are you understanding how important listening is?) In your willingness to listen you are saying to them, "I care about your viewpoint. Your opinions matter. You matter to me. I want to hear what you have to say." You will see the walls begin to come down.

Then, even if the things they have said are offensive to you, if you are slow to speak and respond with pleasant words such as, "I am really sorry you feel that way. That is not in my heart. I care about your development as a part of this ministry. I want to correct whatever is wrong here," your pleasant words set the stage for correction.

WHO, ME?

I used to have a really short fuse. I would "pop off" quickly at someone. Someone would do something, big or small—it didn't matter—and I would be spitting mad, standing an inch from his nose, my flesh wanting to level him.

I had to learn to look at that person in the midst of my anger and say from my heart, "Hey, man, I am really sorry. I did not mean for this to happen. Our relationship is important to me." It is like puncturing a balloon. The pressure is gone almost immediately. Now you have the basis to communicate in a meaningful fashion.

James wrote, **The wisdom that is from above is first pure, then peaceable, gentle, and easy to be intreated, full of mercy and good fruits, without partiality, and without hypocrisy** (James 3:17). Pure refers to something being true.[1] If something is pure, it is not deceitful, manipulative and does not shade the truth. If it is godly, peaceable and gentle, it is pure. It does not provoke wrath or produce hurt or pain.

When you communicate with someone, do it gently. If you're a man, I do not care how macho you think you are, you must learn to be gentle. As I have already said, gentleness is one of the most manly traits in the Bible, but it has been perverted by the world and the Enemy. Being peaceable, gentle and easily entreated—all of these attitudes produce a non-threatening, inoffensive environment for effective communication.

Be Willing To Listen

The Amplified Bible says that wisdom from above is **willing to yield to reason** (James 3:17 AMP). A reasonable person can be easily entreated. You cannot be dogmatic, holding on to your opinions. An effective leader is always willing to yield to reason—not necessarily to the other person—but to reason.

When someone wants to talk to you, be quick to listen. If the point he makes is counter to your opinion or viewpoint, be willing to yield to reason. He knows he is imperfect. He knows he is going to make mistakes. But he will not feel threatened if they know you are a person who moves mercifully in your dealings with people.

THE WORD ON THE SUBJECT

Remember, James 3:17 says true wisdom is **full of mercy and good fruits, without partiality.** You are going to like some people more than others. That is human nature. You are also going to interact more comfortably with some personalities than with others. But if you are going to be an effective communicator, your leadership cannot show partiality one to another. That offends people. It puts up walls and produces a threatening environment. Someone might say, "He likes him better than me. That means I'm going to get the short end of the stick." They begin to read between the lines, and communication is corrupted; loyalty is destroyed.

James 3:17 also says wisdom is without hypocrisy. "You cannot have two standards: one for your followers and one for yourself. What you want to see in them, you must model for them. They will see what you do and have a good example in front of them to follow.

LEARNING TO DEAL WITH ANGRY PEOPLE

To be a person of influence, you must learn to deal with angry people. We live in an angry world where people regularly lose their cool. So how are you going to deal with it?

Proverbs 15:1 says, **A soft answer turneth away wrath: but grievous words stir up anger.** These truths are so simple that most of the time we miss them. I learned this one the hard way.

In 1989, we bought the New Union. It used to be the Union Bar and Grill, where rock music artist Prince made a film. It was a notorious bar, and we bought the place to start a downtown outreach using contemporary Christian music.

I thought the community would love it. After all, a church was replacing one of the most notorious bars in the entire Twin Cities' area. Every night they'd have two or three police calls. It seemed like someone got shot there almost once a week. Dope deals were going down there all the time. Surely the neighborhood should have been grateful that a church had brought them the light of the Gospel and eliminated all that crime and violence. Wrong!

The Setup

The city councilman in charge of our area phoned me and asked, "Would you come to a community meeting and tell us a little bit about yourself and your ministry and what you are going to be contributing to the community?" He sounded really nice. I figured I would go to the community meeting and get a few pats on the back and some warm welcomes for replacing this bar with an outreach center.

So I went to this community meeting and found four or five hundred people jammed into the tiny community center. Channel 5 had their TV camera in the back, and the councilman was already taking full advantage of the publicity for himself. He had been speaking for about half an hour when I arrived.

The Sting

Well, to hear him tell it, we were planning to draw the indigent and homeless from all over the city into their little neighborhood. Vandalism and crime rates were going to skyrocket.

This alderman had these people thoroughly stirred up because they *presumed* that our church came from a nicer rural area into the grimy heart of their city, causing innumerable problems by giving handouts of free food and clothing.

They were ready to tar and feather me.

"No. No. No!" I said. "We are not just going to have soup lines three blocks long to draw indigents. We have a vision to rehabilitate people, and if they are interested in receiving the Word, then we are going to give them a place to live and help them. They'll be doing community service."

It was all very logical. We had a beautiful, well-thought-out plan. But because the people felt threatened, they could not hear anything I said.

The more I tried to defend what we were doing, the worse it got. I had people standing up and using the worst profanity imaginable, calling me every name in the book. Channel 5 was rolling. They were getting all this down for the evening news. I had been set up, big time. But a juicy story like this could not be passed up.

It got so hostile I was not too sure I would get out of the community center in one piece.

A Soft Answer...

Then this verse from Proverbs came to my mind: **A soft answer turneth away wrath.**

So even though I did not feel we had anything to apologize for, I took the microphone and said, "Hey, I am really sorry about this. I should have thought to ask you if our presence in your community would be something you wanted. I should have had a conversation with the councilman here. I should have done these things before we ever bought that property. And please, I ask you to forgive me. I promise you this — we will never set up a soup kitchen in this location, so you do not need to feel threatened about that."

It was not a big thing to give up, because we did not have a soup kitchen in our plan anyway. But the change in my attitude, the apology and the concession on the soup kitchen "popped their anger balloon."

It was one of the most remarkable experiences I have ever had. The whole climate of the meeting changed immediately, and by the time the meeting was over they were shaking my hand, saying, "Welcome to our community. We are glad to have you here." And everything turned out fine.

This is a wonderful example of this truth: sometimes you can diffuse another person's anger. They can be so mad, they are ready to flatten you. But when you say, "Listen, you don't know how sorry I am for inadvertently doing this. I want you to know it is not my heart. I want to have a good relationship with you. I want to be a blessing to you. I am sorry for this," you can almost hear the anger go "pop."

Try this strategy next time you deal with an angry person or group; you will be amazed at how effective it is. And you are preserving a nonthreatening environment, making no room for offense to be taken.

31

FIVE BASIC ESSENTIALS

Webster's dictionary defines *communication* as "the exchange of ideas or information."[1] In biblical terms, the Greek word for communication is *logos*.[2] Colossians 4:6 talks about always letting your speech be seasoned with salt. The word used for *speech* is *logos*. In fact, most of the places in the New Testament where communication or speech is referred to, the Greek word used is *logos*.

With that in mind, turn to John 1:1: **In the beginning was the Word, and the Word was with God, and the Word was God.** Who are we talking about? Jesus, the living Word. Now, guess what the Greek term is for *word* in that verse—*logos,* translated communication and also speech. It is the same word used for Jesus when referred to as the *living* Word. **And the Word was made flesh, and dwelt among us.**

Jesus is the Word made flesh, dwelling among us. In other words, Jesus is God's communication to man of all God is, all God wants for us and all He intends us to be. Jesus is God's communication, His logos, to us.

FULL COMMUNICATION

But understand this—full communication does not take place unless we respond. We have to respond to God's effort to communicate with us through Jesus by opening our hearts to Him and saying, "Jesus, I need You. Come into my life." When we do that, He is communicated to us as God's plan of redemption for our lives.

Salvation has been communicated to us, but it requires a response, or the communication does not take place. If we do not respond to God's effort to communicate, full communication does not happen. This is true on any level. Communication is an *exchange* of thoughts, ideas or information. If an exchange does not take place, if there is no response, communication has not happened. With this new perspective on communication—the successful exchange of information—I want to examine what I believe are five essentials to effective communication.

NUMBER ONE: BE DILIGENT

Be diligent in your effort to communicate with others. Full communication does not happen in many relationships—marriages, for example—because people do not place a priority on communicating, and they do not make the necessary effort. I guarantee you, communication does not happen if a guy gets up in the morning, showers, shaves and dresses, goes to work, comes back ten hours later worn out, picks up the newspaper, eats dinner while he reads, then sits in front of the TV for two hours and goes to bed having said maybe a half dozen words to his wife and kids.

None of us would be the least bit surprised to hear that the relationship had faltered. So the first essential key to communication is that you have to make the effort. You have to be diligent to talk to others. Actually, any relationship you want to cultivate must be approached with diligence: an effort has to be made to talk.

NUMBER TWO: BE A GOOD LISTENER

After diligence, the second key to effective communication is to be a good listener. There are many things you communicate to the other person through good listening. You say to them, "I care enough about you to listen to your point of view and to hear the concerns you are sharing." When you sit and listen to somebody, you are saying to him, "I place my interests in a position secondary to yours. I am going to listen to you and see if I can do something to help you." The act of being a good listener does much to set the stage for effective communication.

As we've read, James 1:19 says, **Wherefore, my beloved brethren, let every man be swift to hear, slow to speak, slow to wrath.** What is number one on his list? Be swift to hear.

NUMBER THREE: MAKE YOUR FIRST RESPONSE POSITIVE

The third essential is to make your first response positive. Make your initial response or, if you are the initiator, your initial comment positive. Proverbs 16:24 says, **Pleasant words are as an honeycomb, sweet to the soul, and health to the bones.** Pleasant words set the stage for someone to hear what you are saying and in turn create the atmosphere for an honest exchange of ideas and information.

This is essential to defusing the threatening environment, bringing down the defensive barriers and opening up the channels of communication.

NUMBER FOUR: BE WILLING TO YIELD TO REASON

The fourth key essential to effective communication is as follows: Do not be dogmatic in your position but instead be willing to yield to reason. If you are dogmatic in the defense of your belief or position, you will cause defensive walls to go up in the other person and you will not communicate effectively. You have to let the other person know you are willing to hear his point of view. Be easily entreated.

NUMBER FIVE: PUT ACTION WITH WORDS

The fifth essential key God put on my heart is to put action with words. You must practice what you preach.

Hypocrisy renders your efforts at communication ineffective. First Thessalonians 1:5 says, **For our gospel came not unto you in word only, but also in power, and in the Holy Ghost, and in much assurance; as ye know what manner of men we were among you for your sake.** In other words, their actions conformed to what they were preaching. Their actions gave meaning to their words and, for that reason, their words came with power.

These are the five basic keys, the basic essentials to effective communication. Be mindful of them. Let the Holy Spirit stir them inside you until they become natural to your personality. Then you can put them out of your mind and focus on where you are going. Then you can press toward the mark God has set before you and your ministry.

32

NEGATIVE PATTERNS OF COMMUNICATION

Negative patterns of communication are a ready retreat for some people. These people are more interested in getting their way or winning an argument than they are in clear and authentic communication. Their negative patterns of attack, defense and manipulation do not leave room for open communication.

Sometimes in a relationship upheaval or during an attempt to communicate, all three of these negative patterns of communication are present and working together.

THE ATTACKER

The attacker creates an environment which inhibits hearing of the truth, even when it is spoken. The Word tells us to speak the truth in love (Eph. 4:15); unfortunately, the attacker simply loves to tell the truth. Sadly, the attacker violates the principle of love by which we are commanded to live.

Oftentimes their behavior is motivated by belief in something that is untrue, which is what makes it impossible for the attacker to communicate truth. He believes the person he is attacking is somehow responsible for the negative circumstance or condition he is facing and that it is the responsibility of the other person to change what the attacker does not like. But our contentment, our satisfaction, is not dependent upon any other human being.

THE SOURCE OF FULFILLMENT

Our fulfillment, contentment and satisfaction with life are not dependent on any other person. If we operate under the misconception of the attacker, we will feel justified in attacking others because we see them as responsible for our discontent. Our satisfaction comes from within. It is the fruit of the reborn human spirit.

Love, joy, peace and long-suffering all reside within you if you are born again, and if they are not coming to the surface of your life, it is no one's fault but your own.

Abe Lincoln had it right when he said, "People are just as happy as they make up their minds to be."[1] The attacker must learn to be more diligent in seeking a spiritual solution to his discontent.

THE IMPOSSIBLE ENVIRONMENT

Besides blaming others for his own dissatisfaction, the attacker also sets up an environment which makes it impossible for others to receive the truth, even when it is spoken, because he sets up a threatening environment.

When someone is attacked, the walls go up. No one is about to bare his soul to someone he feels is a threat to his self-image, security or best interest. If a person feels threatened, communication has been cut off; therefore, the attacker has stopped the very communication he is trying to initiate by virtue of his methods.

NO LOVE HERE

Third, the attacker operates contrary to the principles of love, because when he attacks someone, he is saying, "You are bad. You are evil. You are no good. You blew it. I'm really ticked off at you." The attacker is communicating a message that contradicts what the Bible says about the other person. So on all three accounts, the attacker loses in terms of his choice of communication style.

WHAT IS REALLY HAPPENING?

Attacking behavior is really a response to several things. Let's examine what is really happening behind the behavior by using some examples.

The attacker is doing one of two things.

First, he is feeling some degree of frustration over his present circumstance, and he perceives the source of his discontent within another person. In his attack, he is attempting to communicate—albeit not well—his desire for change to that other person.

Second, an attack will occur because the attacker perceives he is being attacked. His best method of defense is to launch a counterattack. He figures his best defense is a strong offense.

BILL AND LAURA

Here's an example of how this works. Let's say Bill was supposed to fix a dripping faucet for the last several weeks and has not gotten around to it. His wife Laura is totally fed up with the delay, and she lets him know as much one evening. She says, "I can't stand it anymore! This dripping faucet is driving me right up a wall. When are you going to fix it?"

Bill perceives he is being attacked and immediately counterattacks, saying, "Well, how am I going to have time to fix the faucet when I'm busy doing all your other errands? I just got through taking your mama home down in Redwood Falls. It took me half the day to get her down there!"

Laura says, "So now you're harping about my mama. I asked you to take my mom to Redwood Falls, and you said you would. Now you are using that against me. You are just trying to pick a fight!"

Bill says, "I'm not trying to pick a fight—I'm just trying to tell you why I didn't have time to fix the faucet. You expect too much out of me."

Laura says, "Expect too much out of you! What do you expect out of me? Look at all the things I do, and you never even say thank you."

I could go on, but you get the idea. They have totally forgotten what even started the discussion. After the first comment it became a case of attack and counterattack.

COMMUNICATING THE TRUTH IN LOVE

The whole incident would never have gone that way had Laura done what the Bible says to do, which is to communicate the truth in love.

If she had said, "Bill, I know you have been really busy, and I realize there have been a lot of demands on your time. I know that is why the faucet has not been fixed yet, but it really is bothering me. I'm wondering if there's something I could do to relieve the pressure on you so you could work on the faucet."

Laura was uptight about the faucet not being fixed, but she can communicate that in a way that does not get Bill "fired up."

Now, on the other hand, if Bill had known how to react, he would have said something like this when Laura attacked: "Honey, I realize the faucet is a point of frustration for you, and I apologize for not having fixed it. I'll do my best to make time to fix it tomorrow." And the whole fight would have been defused.

On the Receiving End

Now, when you are on the other end of an attack, how do you respond? How do you reply so you can get communication back on a plane where it can be productive? The Bible says a soft answer turns away wrath. So if you are attacked and someone lets you have both barrels, what do you do? Say, "I'm sorry; I didn't mean to do that, and I apologize. Please forgive me. I'll really work on that problem."

What do you want? Do you want the plan of God in that relationship, or do you want to win the argument? That is really the bottom line. Your flesh wants to win the argument. But if you want what God wants, if you want a solid relationship He can use to bring ministry to you and through you, then you cannot allow the flesh to decide the issue for you. You will have to forego winning the argument in favor of allowing the Spirit of God to cause you to give a soft answer.

The Defender

The second type or pattern of negative communication is to become defensive. I have had people say, "You should focus a little bit more on the guy who is so offensive. After all, if he had been a little bit more diplomatic in the way he said things, the offense would never have occurred."

But you cannot do anything about the attacker. You cannot change him. You can only do something about the way you respond to the attack.

It is a fact that every time there is division, every time there is a split, every time a relationship has difficulty and deteriorates, it is because people have gotten offended. They have "taken their marbles" and gone home.

It does not make any difference how justified we may be. If we allow ourselves to be offended or to become defensive, then we are lining up with the Devil instead of God. We are being vessels available to the wrong force, bringing division to the body of Christ. We have to understand how abominable it is to God when we participate in anything which divides the body of Christ.

This defensive attitude keeps people from receiving legitimate admonishment and correction. Defensiveness makes people unteachable and perpetuates error in their lives.

Lastly, defensiveness is dangerous because it rejects God's desire to be our recompense. God says He wants to vindicate you. (Heb. 10:30.)

CREATED FOR RIGHT RELATIONSHIPS

God created us to be in right relationships, not only with Him but with other people. There may be some who say, "Not me. I don't need other people. I don't need relationships. I'm independent." That is just a reaction to a fear of being rejected. So they step back from relationships which might result in rejection.

Because of the way God made us, every human longs for, needs and is motivated by a desire to be accepted and loved by other people. But we live in a world that is geared in the other direction. Rejection is the status quo. The world only offers acceptance as a condition of good performance. If people do not perform, they may be rejected, demoted, fired, kicked out, divorced, imprisoned or maybe even executed.

So when we are confronted with the possibility of rejection, we become defensive. This defensiveness is nothing more than a process of self-justification to avoid the pain of rejection. To justify our behavior in hopes of avoiding rejection, we say things like, "Well, I did this because of that circumstance. I didn't really do anything wrong because...."

A Family Tradition

Many people have grown up in a family where the attack/defend syndrome was all they knew. They grew up in a family where they were attacked from the time they were old enough to understand English. So they became chronic defenders. Eventually they defend themselves even when there is no legitimate attack taking place. To an extreme, they become people you cannot say anything to without them taking offense.

With all this attacking/defending going on we wonder why we have so many splits and divisions in the body of Christ. Well, offense is the issue, because without the tendency to become offended, there would never be any division in the body of Christ.

Just think, if all the churches in your city were in unity, no one was offended about anyone else's doctrine but everyone had the same mind and the same purpose of seeing the community changed by God for the better, your city would be changed by now. We must learn to fight the temptation to be defensive, because it only makes us "putty" in the hands of the Devil and cripples the body of Christ.

Unconditionally and Eternally Accepted

God has said that in Jesus Christ you are unconditionally and eternally accepted by Him (1 Peter 2:5), so that is all that matters. Having that understanding is the first step to avoiding the temptation to be defensive in our dealings with people on a day-to-day basis.

We must have a clear understanding of how to deal with defensiveness. We must understand that divided relationships on any level are an abomination to God. If we allow ourselves to be party to division or divided relationships, we are well out of the will of God. We cannot expect His protection, His blessing or His provision in our lives. When we really have a revelation of that truth, then we will not allow ourselves to become offended when someone says something to us the wrong way.

Instead of erecting our own defense in a matter, we should rely on our heavenly Father to justify us. If you do not become defensive and you rely on and trust in His Word, He says He will be your recompense, He will vindicate you and every tongue that has risen against you in judgment, you will condemn. In Isaiah 54:17 God promises that to you.

THE MANIPULATOR

The American Heritage Dictionary says that manipulation is the control of or playing upon another person or group of people through artful, unfair or insidious means.[2] In other words, it is an attempt to control another's behavior through deception.

Even by Webster's definition we can see that *manipulation* is morally wrong, can we not? It will absolutely destroy a relationship.

The Bible does not use the term manipulation, but it talks about manipulation quite a bit. Ephesians 4:14 says, **Henceforth be no more children, tossed to and fro, and carried about with every wind of doctrine, by the sleight of men, and cunning craftiness, whereby they lie in wait to deceive.** Deception is an essential ingredient of manipulation.

Look at Ephesians 5:6. Again we see a similar admonition from Scripture. **Let no man deceive you with vain** [empty or meaningless] **words.** That is what manipulation does. It is deceiving someone by communicating in such a way as to cover the true intention or motive, with the goal of exacting a desired response from the other person.

MANIPULATION VS. DECEPTION

Now understand this: not all deception is manipulation. But all manipulation involves deception. The key distinction between the two is whether or not the deception is for the purpose of controlling someone's behavior. A lot of deception does not have control as a motive. But any deception that is entered into willfully or knowingly for the purpose of controlling another person's behavior is manipulation.

Here is what the manipulator thinks: *That guy will never respond like I want him to if I just level with him. So I'll just doctor up my communication a little bit to get him to do what I want him to do.*

Even God does not impose Himself on our ability to make our own decisions unhindered, but the manipulator, through deception, does. That is why it is so destructive to relationships. Even if the manipulator is successful in getting the behavioral change he desires and even if the other person does not realize he is being manipulated, it will destroy the relationship.

> *The truth is, nobody is going to change unless it happens in the heart first. True, lasting change is only a result of the Holy Spirit's interaction . . .*

The truth is, nobody will change unless it happens in the heart first. True, lasting change is only a result of the Holy Spirit's interaction with our spirits. This causes us to have a change of heart. So it is an erroneous assumption that manipulation can bring about a change in someone else's behavior.

THE OTHER SIDE OF THE COIN

If you are on the other side of the coin, you are the one who is being manipulated, and you have just as much responsibility to take corrective action as the other person. Don't point your finger at him and say, "Well, he's the one doing the manipulating. He has the problem."

No, you cannot stop someone's manipulative behavior any more than you can stop someone whose communication style is to attack. However, just as with the attacker, you can do something about your response and the way you deal with manipulation. The Word of God says not to let anyone deceive you, because the will of God for your life cannot be realized if you are controlled by someone else's desires.

MANIPULATION VS. PERSUASION

Let me clarify that it is not wrong to want to convince someone to do something for you. It is not wrong to persuade someone to see things from your point of view. It is not wrong to be an agent of change in someone else's life. That is not manipulation.

As a matter of fact, what we are doing when we preach the gospel to all the world is simply persuading people to another point of view. When we present the gospel to people who do not know Jesus and we confront them with His reality and the place He desires to have in their lives, we do so as a Holy Spirit-directed agent of change in their lives. We are praying and believing that we can have an impact on them which will affect not only the way they think, but the way they act.

So it is not wrong to want to be an agent of change in someone else's life or to persuade someone to see your point of view. The way you go about it is what determines whether it is manipulation or persuasion.

If you communicate openly, laying out all the options on the table and telling the truth in a loving way without pressuring others to make a decision, then you haven't manipulated anyone.

KEYS TO IDENTIFYING MANIPULATION

There are three keys which will help you identify manipulation when it occurs in your life. You can use these keys either for the purpose of determining whether you are manipulating others or others are manipulating you.

The first key is that manipulation is the imposition of obligation on others, usually through condemnation or guilt. The Bible says there is only one thing we are obligated to do regarding another person: **Owe no man any thing, but to love one another.** (Rom. 13:8). That means our only obligation to other people is to love them.

Now that covers a wide range of things. The Bible does say we are obligated to do what we do for our employer as unto the Lord (Col. 3:23), to give him the same level of commitment and effort we would give to Jesus Himself. Ephesians 5:25 says husbands are obligated to love their wives like Christ loves His church, and wives are obligated to revere their husbands as their head and to submit to him as to the Lord. (vv. 22–23.)

Now, any obligation that does not fall within the parameters of the Word of God has been imposed on you through condemnation or guilt. That guilt is imposed through obligatory statements, and it does not matter whether someone else says them to you or you say them to yourself.

How do you identify an obligatory statement? They will always contain the words *should, ought* or *must*. When you hear those words, your antenna ought to go up, because, chances are, an obligation is soon to follow.

THE EMOTIONAL PLOY

The second key is identifying anything that plays on a person's emotions in order to exact a particular response. Emotions are designed to give us impetus in the decisions we make, not to be the basis for our decisions. So when someone starts playing on our emotions to force a desired behavior or response, that is manipulation.

When a spouse is intimidated by their mate's temper, they are being manipulated. The manipulator uses their anger to keep their spouse at a distance, forcing them to relate in a particular way to avoid an angry outburst. That is emotional manipulation.

The spouse who gives their mate the silent treatment is also a manipulator, withholding relationship to get what he or she wants or to show disapproval. These blatant examples of manipulation take place every day, and they can destroy a relationship.

USING THE WORD OF GOD DECEITFULLY

The third key to discerning manipulation, and the most important for Christians, is recognizing when the Word of God is being used deceitfully.

Therefore seeing we have this ministry, as we have received mercy, we faint not; but have renounced the hidden things of dishonesty, not walking in craftiness [or manipulation]**, nor handling the word of God deceitfully; but by manifestation of the truth commending ourselves to every man's conscience in the sight of God.**

2 Corinthians 4:1,2

I can't think of a worse form of deception— the Word God can set people free or put someone in bondage according to one's desires. It must be a stench in the nostrils of God when that happens.

One of the most serious forms of using the Word deceitfully relates to ministries and money appeals. We have all received letters in the mail with a lot of underlined words saying, "If we do not receive your money today, the ministry is going to face some dire consequence or possibly go down the drain."

Listen, God does not manipulate, and we don't have to either. God is perfectly capable of getting the finances to the people who will use them as He wants them used. Perhaps the ministries that whine about "going off the air unless you send money" should go off the air. Then there would be room for another ministry that teaches people how to have faith in God to supply their needs.

If God has called a ministry to do something, He is going to provide for it. And if He does not provide for it, He did not call them to do it. Period!

Now there is nothing manipulative about a ministry or person presenting a legitimate need, but you can make needs known to people without emotionally manipulating them. In addition, the Bible tells us not to respond to emotional appeals.

Paul indicates that emotional appeals create feelings of resentment because we know we have been manipulated: **Every man according as he purposeth in his heart, so let him give; not grudgingly, or of necessity** [the Amplified says under compulsion]: **for God loveth a cheerful giver** (2 Cor. 9:7).

> *If God has called a ministry to do something, He is going to provide for it. And if He does not provide for it, He did not call them to do it. Period!*

Manipulation in Christian circles often does involve handling the Word of God deceitfully, which means they use the Word to bring benefit to themselves in one way or another.

Know the seriousness of manipulation. Don't allow it to happen. The solution is very simple. Remember our definition of effective communication: speaking the truth in love.

WHAT TO DO, WHAT TO DO

If you have identified yourself as a manipulator (a very difficult thing to admit), then know that the greatest way to walk in love with people is to give them every unhindered opportunity to exercise their freedom of choice without pressuring them.

If you are the one who has been manipulated, know that speaking the truth in love is the cure for it. In a loving way, you have to truthfully show that person that he is communicating in a way which is harmful to your relationship, causing you to be resentful and angry. Say, "Look, let's approach this another way." And then deal with the questions honestly. Speaking the truth in love solves the problems of manipulation. It is not always easy or comfortable, but it works.

SECTION 4

The Mandate To Motivate

33

DELEGATE TO MOTIVATE

Right after I got out of the military, my family and I moved to Meridian, Mississippi, and I bought a little aviation business. One of the guys I was teaching to fly was the founder of Peavey Electronics, one of the world's most successful, most profitable businesses in the electronics arena. I used to look at him and wonder how in the world he could do so well, because he seemed to violate so many leadership principles; but he was one of the best people-motivators I have ever met.

If we do not do things to motivate the people God has brought to us, the ministry will not perform in a way consistent with God's plan. So you have to become not only a visionary, not only a communicator, but also a motivator. Your leadership must ignite the fires of enthusiasm and excitement within the people who work for you.

Over the years, I have looked at people who have succeeded in group or corporate efforts and wondered, *What is he doing anyway? He doesn't look like he has things together very well, but somehow, he*

seems to extract 110 percent from the people who are working for him,
and he has more success than anyone else.

A MARGIN FOR SUCCESS

Being a good motivator allows you to make up for a lot of other failures. You can blow it in a few of the other areas, but if you are a good motivator, if you can get people to give you 110 percent, then you will be on top. Good motivation skills give you a margin for success.

We want to progress from the positional authority God gives us for being faithful and diligent to being a relationally skilled leader, someone people want to follow. Then we want to be an operationally skilled leader, a person who can produce the kind of fruit that gets people excited about what they are doing. And then we want to move into the highest level of leadership development: becoming a leader who establishes an organization in which the people's gifts can be matured and come to fruition.

These levels of leadership development can best be achieved by a visionary, a communicator and a motivator.

ORGANIZATION AS A BASIS FOR MOTIVATION

The way you organize your philosophy of management has much to do with your ability to motivate people.

In Exodus 18:19-20 Jethro, Moses' father-in-law, says, "Moses, you can't possibly personally direct, minister to and pastor two million murmuring Jews. You can't do it. You are going to need some help in this matter." So Moses built the first organizational pyramid.

Verse 21 says he appointed rulers of thousands, rulers of hundreds, rulers of fifties and rulers of tens. God still gave the direction for the children of Israel to Moses, but now he had a method of disseminating information and motivating people to follow the leadership he was ordained to provide—through this organizational pyramid.

How does the pyramid communicate? Through delegation. He delegated authority and responsibility. Those two things must go hand in hand. Many people try to delegate responsibility, but then hold on to the authority themselves.

If you are going to have people working for you, you will need to delegate both the responsibility and the authority to do what you have called them to do. The best manager is an effective delegator, someone who can identify a gift in others and give them the responsibility, that will enable their gifts to grow.

THE BEST USE OF YOUR TIME

When you delegate, you free up your own time for creative thought and prayer. A leader has to invest his best effort to allow for time to hear from God, to get the direction from the Lord to plan and strategize. Someone has to think about that.

Most people in the organization are task-oriented, doing the things they have been given to do. It is the job of leadership to think, plan and let the Holy Spirit put all the pieces together.

As a leader on any level of authority, if you make it possible for the Spirit of God to show you how to be productive by thinking, praying and giving Him time, He will "blow the lid off" your department with growth. That will not be possible, however, unless you learn to delegate. You have to come to a place where you can take your hands off the day-to-day things.

PROVING THE CONCEPT

I had a lot of difficulty with this concept earlier in my life. After we bought the aviation business, I started an air freight company. We grew rapidly, and over a period of about three years, we added fifty pilots, fifty mechanics, fifty or so ramp agents and a number of administrative people. I had 150 to 200 employees, and I was trying to do everything for everyone.

I had a chief pilot, but I didn't really need him because I did all of his duties. I got in his way. I had a director of operations, but I didn't really need him; I did all of his duties, too. Our director of maintenance might just as well have turned wrenches, because I took care of everything else. And every time I visited a city, I was in everyone's way. I was doing everything.

APPLICATION TO MINISTRY

When I went into the ministry, the Lord said, "If you have prayed about it and you believe you have hired the people I told you to hire, then take your hands off of their responsibilities. Let them do what I have anointed them to do. They are anointed to do it, hot shot! Not you! [Ouch!] It is your responsibility to be a resource to them in the performance of their duty."

"Yes, Sir!" I said. This is the heart of delegation.

People who have come to work for this ministry have said to me, "Boy, you sure are a hands-off manager. We don't see you very much. What do you do, by the way?" I am doing my own job, but the Lord's instruction to me was to let those anointed to do a job do it.

One of the reasons I keep the schedule I do is so that I can keep my hands off better if I'm not there. When I make an appearance in the office area, I can get sidetracked very easily and start doing things I should not be involved in. So for the most part it is easier for me if I just do not show up. Both my sons think I have a soft job. It doesn't mean I don't work. I am doing my part by keeping my hands off. Delegation means you entrust people with authority and responsibility, you do not micromanage.

DELEGATING THE APPROACH

One of the things I want for the managers in our ministry is for them to learn the same hands-off approach. They have to view themselves in a management capacity as a resource to the people who are working for them. Their job is to help those people if they have problems or questions or need a little motivation or advice. A good leader will give encouragement, exhortation as well as the benefit of his or her experience. It is not your job as a leader to micromanage.

Free up your time to do what is really essential, the things only you as the manager can do, like the planning and hearing from the Spirit regarding strategy, long-range and short-range plans. When you entrust people with the responsibility and the authority you have delegated to them, you are making demands on the gifts of God in them—the *only* demands which can cause them to grow.

> *One of the things I want for the managers in our ministry is for them to learn the same hands-off approach.*

This is the primary way you help to develop the gifts of God in others. Sometimes it is not an easy thing to do.

I have had the Lord tell me to release a particular area of responsibility to people. I battled in my mind, arguing with God. "Lord, they are not ready for this; they will cause a disaster for sure. I do not believe they are in a place where they can do this." But I would get that continual, persistent nudging in that direction, so I would give in to God and delegate the responsibility to them.

Time and again, I have watched the Lord lift those people to a new level of performance. They have grown in a way they would not have otherwise. It is tempting to take credit for their growth, but the Lord keeps me humble by reminding me I was only being an obedient delegator.

BE THE QUARTERBACK

A good quarterback usually hands the football to someone else who is responsible to gain yardage. He will either hand off to a running back or pass to a receiver.

Always be looking for things you can hand off to someone else—and not just the awful jobs you don't want to do. Like a good quarterback, hand off the tasks which will develop the talent in your "receivers." You are developing the gifts of God in them; let them take credit for the "winning touchdown."

I hear people say, "Well, it's a shame, but as the organization grows, you reach the limit of people's capabilities. You have to fire them and get others in order to progress any further." No. That is inconsistent with the Word of God. Growing ministries or businesses do not have to reach the limit of the staff's capabilities.

Blend your willingness to make every educational opportunity available to the people who work for you. Encourage them to develop their natural gifts and talents, and then entrust them with additional responsibilities as the Lord gives you direction. You will see them grow into newer and larger arenas of responsibility than ever before. And as they grow, your organization will grow from within.

ASKING FOR TROUBLE

One of the ways you can open yourself to a lot of difficulties as a leader is to hire from outside your organization. You end up with people who have never known your vision, do not understand you and have no particular loyalty to you. If they are managers, there is a potential for division and difficulty. It is always best to staff from within the organization, to raise people up from inside.

When opportunities for advancement are available, you must understand the principles of delegation and encouragement, which staff members need to grow into higher levels of responsibility. Then your willingness to trust God's direction for them will produce the most solid organization.

When you do that, you have their hearts. They understand that God has used you and your organization to bring them to a place they would not otherwise have reached. And you have a loyal bunch now.

It is the hands-off approach that is most consistent with the Word of God. The Bible says a man's gift makes room for him. (Prov. 18:16.) So you take your hands off and trust God to use the gifts within that individual to bring about the results you desire. Delegate to motivate!

34

THE FAITH OF EXPECTATION

W hen you genuinely expect an employee to rise to the highest standard of performance imaginable, it has the supernatural effect of pulling him there. In Jeremiah 29:11 God says he has prepared for you an expected end.

If you are a leader and expect all of your people to perform to a high standard in order to achieve what God has called you to do, you will see something like a supernatural hand reaching down and pulling them to a higher level of performance than otherwise might have been possible. I see this on virtually every level of authority.

There have been extensive studies done in the area of parent/child relationships which reflect this truth: a child will rise no higher in a level of achievement than his parents' expectations. There have been examples of children with IQ's in the genius range who never make it out of school because their parents told them they were stupid or weren't going to amount to anything. Poor expectation by the parents yielded poor performance by the child.

In some instances a mentor figure in a child's life, other than the parent, is able to raise a child's performance with his or her expectations. But basically what parents expect from their children will determine how they perform and what they accomplish in life.

I am not interested in allowing a nonperformer the luxury of blaming his parents' low expectations for his life. Yes, it does have an effect; however, every individual chooses the quality of his life. My point is, your expectations as a leader can supernaturally impact the performance of those who work for you. Your expectations are critical to their performance.

PREJUDICED BY THE PAST

Here is a challenge we must all overcome. What are our expectations generally based upon? Past performance, right? For us to expect to experience the promise of God instead of what is in the world, we have to deliberately exercise our faith in the promise of God. And yet, where our relationships are concerned, we let others' mistakes predispose us to the same attitude toward them rather than employing one of our greatest tools—the expectation of faith—to lift them up. So when someone has not done as well as you would have liked him to do, do not fall into the trap of "writing him off." Your expectation of better things for him could be the very thing which will lift him up.

THE GENUINE ARTICLE

Now, this expectation has to be genuine. You cannot simply go to someone saying, "I believe you're really going to do well this quarter," trying to pull on this scriptural truth like a slot machine, hoping for the jackpot of better performance. No. Your expectations for this person must really be in your heart. There is only one way you can get to that place. The apostle Paul gave us the model in the prayers for his followers.

Paul prayed that the church at Ephesus would have a revelation of the hope of God's calling and of the exceeding greatness of His power toward those who believe. (Eph. 1:18,19.) When you pray in faith and believe your prayers are going to get results, that elevates your expectation, does it not?

As a leader, one of the most important things you can do is pray in that manner over the people God has called to work for you. Pray the same way Paul prayed over the church at Ephesus—in faith, believing God for His best. It will elevate your expectation of what those individuals can do. Then, from a heart filled with faith, you can encourage them to strive for loftier heights and goals than they ever have before. Your encouragement will be genuine. You really will believe they can do it.

DIVIDED VISION

One of the most destabilizing, momentum-robbing influences in an organization is divided vision.

Habakkuk 2:2 says, **Write *the* vision, and make it plain upon tables, that he may run that readeth it.** *The* vision means the vision which describes the focus of your effort in the Kingdom of God. It isn't a multiple vision. The principle from Scripture is that you are to be single-minded. If you have diverse interests and diverse visions, the effort will be divided, loyalties will be divided and productivity will be minimized. One of the most important things any organization can do is to make sure the people have singleness of heart and mind in what they are called to do.

A LESSON LEARNED

On one or two occasions I have allowed someone to come on staff who has said something like, "Pastor, I do a little graphic arts work on the side. My focus is the church, but I have this little business which supplements my income. Do you mind?" At the time I didn't mind, but I learned a lesson. The business divided the person's vision and his effort. It robbed his impetus, momentum and motivation. He was unable to put all of his energy toward his purpose in the Kingdom and into our ministry.

When people accumulate a fair amount of time off, the temptation is to use their time or their skills to generate additional income. That seems harmless, but it divides their vision, divides their interest and ultimately divides their loyalty to the organization. Plus it robs them of some much-needed rest. I have seen the Enemy use this technique to subvert and undermine ministries.

Every organization has to come to a point where the leaders say, "Okay, we're not going to allow this, because it enables the Enemy to divide the attention of our people and produce something contrary to the ministry's and the people's best interest."

Individuals who work for you might say, "This isn't fair. I had a chance to use my skills to develop some extra income and bring an extra measure of blessing to my family." That should not concern you. If you are being faithful to the ministry where God has called you, your obedience will bring His supernatural power to meet your need. You will not have to help God take care of you!

The same thing can happen when someone has a ministry effort of his own, separate from the ministry which employs him. Jesus said a man cannot serve two masters. (Luke 16:13.) As leaders in an organization of the Kingdom, we must work to bring a single-minded purpose to our department or our area of ministry. The ministry's success and the individual's success both will be enhanced by that single-mindedness.

God Is Able

Jesus said when you are faithful in what is another man's, He will give you that which is your own. (Luke 16:12.) But that faithfulness includes more than showing up for a forty-hour workweek. Your heart must get involved. You are the only one who can put your heart into a particular place. And faithfulness is described as the place where you put your heart's effort—your time, your vision, your faith—and where God connects you in the performance of ministry.

Jesus said that when you are faithful there, He will promote you. (Luke 16:10.) But faithfulness is the key. So don't allow the Enemy to divide your interest or your vision. It robs momentum; it robs motivation.

MISPLACED LOYALTIES

You have an obligation as a leader in ministry to always orient the loyalties of those who work under you toward the ministry and not toward you. You are the one who has frequent contact with them, the one they are going to learn to like and respect as they work with you every day. If you are cultivating the relationship properly, trust is going to grow. Be very deliberate in making sure their loyalties are not misplaced on you. It has to be toward the ministry and the vision of the ministry. Our obligation is to the larger body of Christ.

Our highest obligation is to Jesus. He is the Head of the church, the Head of the body. Our obligation is to the corporate body. Misplaced loyalties undermine momentum and motivation.

Let me give you an example. Our music minister was with Oral Roberts University for eight years before he came to us. He was Richard Roberts' piano player. He developed a lot of the music ministry at ORU. He had some wonderful musicians he was laboring to draw into our church.

Recently we had an opportunity to hire a man for our music department whose credentials would make your mouth water. But it became apparent to me that he desired to join our staff because of his loyalty to my music minister, not because he felt any connection with our church.

I didn't know him from Adam's house cat. He had no loyalties to us at all; however, he had a lot of loyalty to my music minister. Praise God, I had the wisdom not to add him to our staff. Be sure you take an active part in properly shaping the loyalties of the people who work for you.

CONTROLLING STRIFE AND DIVISION

Strife and division within the ministry are the biggest momentum and motivation robbers there are. Therefore, one of your highest responsibilities organizationally is to make sure they do not occur. What have we said time and again? How can two walk together except they be agreed? There must be concord and harmony. The principle of successful ministry is to strive together for the faith to spread the gospel. Anything which undermines that togetherness, which promotes division and contention within the ministry, has to be dealt with quickly. Nip it in the bud. But be sure to have the faith of expectation over those who work for you; it lifts them to a higher level and promotes loyalty in your organization like nothing else.

35

MOTIVATION BY REWARD

How do we motivate people to give us their best effort 100 percent of the time without becoming "clockwatchers"?

The single greatest management principle has been said to be this: The things that bring reward are the things that get done. Simple, isn't it? Things are not going to get done because of our wonderful personalities or because we are such great leaders. The keys to successful behavior are praises and raises.

We have a lot of strange ideas about what motivates people, but the truth is, rewards motivate people. That scriptural truth was confirmed in Philippians 3:14: **I press toward the mark for the prize of the high calling of God in Christ Jesus.**

The high calling of God in Christ Jesus is the high ministry purpose, the lofty dream, the goal Paul was shooting for. He did not say he would press toward that. He said he was pressing toward *the mark*, an intermediate objective, that would take him in that direction.

But what motivated him to press on? He said, **I press toward the mark for *the prize*.** Some translations actually use the word *reward*. There is a reward in reaching the high calling of God. It is a reward of divine provision and blessing not found anywhere else. Because the principle of reward is scriptural, it works in any arena of corporate endeavor. The people who give you the most are frequently the people you reward the most.

THE WRONG IDEA

One of the reasons that many ministries have never been very successful is that they have the mentality that they work for God for nothing. They think that if you are not willing to do the Lord's work for free, you are in it for the wrong reason or your heart isn't right. That simply is not true. God says in Luke 10:7, **the labourer is worthy of his hire.**

Now, there are many different ways to reward people. There are many ways you can motivate with rewards that are not necessarily monetary. Let's look at some of them, including salary.

MONEY

Salary schedules may not be something you have the latitude to freely use as a reward. They may already be set; however, the good news is there are many other ways you can reward people.

Money should be tied to employees' performance as they reach the goals and objectives they have set. Let them know that the annual review, which is a look at their performance in regard to those objectives, is what determines their raise—whether they get one at all and how much.

RECOGNITION, PRAISE AND AFFIRMATION

What I believe works effectively for most leaders and managers is praise, the recognition and the affirmation you give your employees for their work.

I would rather have someone tell me that one of my sermons ministered to him or her than receive a dozen Christmas presents without a word said. The affirmation that my effort produced a desired result in someone else's life means more to me than I can describe, and I know I am not unique in that. We are all made that way; those words of affirmation are a reinforcement of our value.

> We are all valuable in the sight of God because of Christ Jesus, and our self-esteem and our self-worth should not depend on what we do.

We are all valuable in the sight of God because of Christ Jesus, and our self-esteem and our self-worth should not depend on what we do. But the fact remains that it is good to be affirmed that we are moving down the right path. It is good for someone to say, "You are doing a good job. I want you to know I appreciate you. You are a godsend to me and a blessing to my life. Thank you for the effort you have made."

When you learn to use positive affirmation like that, recognizing and praising people for their efforts, and you do it from your heart, you have done as much to motivate them as anything you can do.

THE MINIMUM DAILY REQUIREMENT

Managers who have worked to develop their "people skills" have learned this lesson well. They know how to recognize and positively affirm the behavior which produces positive results. They compliment regularly, because they know one cannot praise someone too much if it is from the heart. If your praise is an artificial thing, then one time is too much. But if it is from the heart, you cannot tell people too often how special they are.

Hebrews 10:24 tells us we are to exhort, encourage and admonish one another to love and good works. Praise is a motivational tool you should not ignore.

Extra Time Off

Another way you can reward people is with extra time off. That can be a real blessing. I'm not saying every time they do a certain thing they should get a day off. But every now and then, if you have the authority from your superior to do this, just go up to someone who has been working hard and been faithful and say, "Hey, take a day off tomorrow. Be blessed. Go play golf. Get in the Word. Go to a seminar." This is a significant way to say thank you and to positively reinforce the contribution he has made and to encourage him to continue.

A Piece of the Action

A third way to reward people is to give them "a piece of the action." In the business world that might mean giving them stock in the company. Secular studies have shown that companies which have more than thirty percent of their ownership invested in their employees produce seventy-five percent more than similar companies which do not. Ownership is a powerful, motivating factor.

Well, how do we do that in a nonprofit organization? How do we make people owners? Very basically, we let them have not only responsibility but recognition for a certain ministry thrust within that organization. Tell them, "Okay, this is your baby. It's all yours. Run with it."

Then six months later when they have done a wonderful job, have them stand up in front of the rest of the group and publicly acknowledge the effort they have made and thank them for what they have done.

By giving them the responsibility for that area of ministry and then liberally recognizing the successes they've achieved, you have made them an "owner." They have stock in the company. There may not be a financial piece of the company available, but there certainly is ownership in terms of recognizing their success.

PROMOTION AS A REWARD

Promotion, of course, is a reward. Promotion can literally be to a higher position or it can be in the sense of increased responsibility. People respond well to increased responsibility. If they are people who are success-oriented to any degree, then it is a meaningful reward for them. This one is a reward for me, too, because it means I have less to do, and it allows me to focus my attention on other issues. It's a double blessing.

PERSONAL GROWTH OPPORTUNITIES

As employees become increasingly valuable to your organization, it is good to make personal growth opportunities available to them. Pay for them to attend seminars in their area of work or classes which will positively impact their work performance or their sense of personal satisfaction. One such example would be the Dale Carnegie people-skills seminars. Warning: avoid seminars which involve metaphysics.

LITTLE THINGS MEAN A LOT

There are other little things you can do, such as planning special events together. If you are a leader responsible for a number of people, it is good to invite them over to your house occasionally and have a little get-together. Learn when their birthdays are and send them cards. Send them Christmas cards. Be aware of the things going on in their lives that are important to them.

Personalize the cards you send them with a note, saying, "Thank you for your effort. I appreciate the part you are playing in my life and ministry. God bless you." Do it sincerely, or it can become offensive. If it is obviously insincere, it looks like manipulation. Let it be something which emanates from your heart. It is just another way of rewarding and saying thank you.

It's Worth the Time

Rewards are the most basic motivational influence we can exert on the people in our organization who are accountable to us. Become reward-minded and see that the greatest means for dispensing rewards is your mouth.

The affirmation, the encouragement, the exhortation, the praise, the recognition—all of these are ways to show the people who work for you how important they are to you. Pray about ways to reward them which will have special meaning to them. Let God show you how to be more affirming of the good things they do, because it will create the kind of behavior you want within your organization.

36

REWARDING RIGHT BEHAVIOR

W hen you hire a new employee, you must make sure he understands what is important to you. Let him know he is going to be rewarded accordingly.

Often one mistake we make in leadership is that we reward the wrong kind of behavior. We reward non-productive behavior and ignore the behavior that gets results. So what kind of behaviors deserve reward?

LOYALTY

Loyalty is the foundation of any organization's or ministry's success. Loyalty reduces turnover. Loyalty promotes longevity of employees, enabling you to develop the skills, as time passes, which make them more effective. Loyalty allows you to cultivate leaders for future growth and expansion. Loyalty is the foundation of long-term, long-range success. Loyalty should be rewarded.

PERSONAL GROWTH

Sometimes, as a reward, our ministry will send people who have been faithful and diligent to school. This will enhance their skill level and give them a broader educational base, making them more useful in the plan of God. You should always reward a person who takes the initiative to pursue personal growth.

Many times people in leadership will take vacation time to go to seminars and do things which promote personal growth. That kind of interest, understanding and awareness should always be rewarded, especially during their review each year, if it has helped them meet their goals and objectives.

CREATIVITY

In doing the same job day in and day out, dealing with the same people, it is easy to get "in the box" of mindless work. This causes you to establish patterns of habitual behavior. You will then fall into the trap of mindless conformity which, perhaps at one time, was productive or efficient. As the organization grows, you are going to have to change. Mindless conformity never contributes to growth. Creativity does.

There should be a reward for applied creativity. People often come up with new ways of doing things more efficiently. They will have ideas which produce what Proverbs 8:12 calls "witty inventions." Some of these ideas may be very innovative and reach a whole new segment of people with the message of Jesus or enhance the efficiency of the organization. Reward those ideas.

SOLID SOLUTIONS TO PROBLEMS

As a leader, you are a problem solver. You will often deal with unforeseen contingencies. If all you had to do was lay out a program of action, you could do that; review your employees once a year for performance and rewards and stay home the rest of the year. But you are a resource to them and should help solve problems when they happen, every day of every workweek.

High on any organization's list of desired behavior are solid solutions to problems. Too often, there are quick-fix artists. Something happens, you need a quick fix, and someone takes care of it. But that is not really what is important. What is important is finding a long-term solution to the challenge you have just faced.

> *High on any organization's list of desired behavior are solid solutions to problems. Too often, there are quick-fix artists.*

Accordingly, you must evaluate people and programs over a reasonably long period of time. We tend to make judgments too quickly. Someone makes an effort and fails, and we are sometimes a little too quick in our judgment.

Your first response to those under you who do not perform well should be to offer them your assistance. Maybe all they need are the resources you can offer. If not, offer correction, help them understand the changes they should make in order to correct the failure and give them a period of time to reevaluate the sum of their efforts.

When your employees know you are looking for the long-term solution rather than the quick fix, they are more inclined to produce solid solutions to problems. That kind of behavior should be rewarded.

RISK TAKING

There are maintainers, and there are go-getters. Some people have their heads so buried that they cannot see opportunity. They are task-oriented, and sometimes the opportunity for something really good escapes them. Others might see the opportunity, but are too timid to take the risk of going after it.

Then there are people who just seem to be able to make things happen. They see and they seize opportunities. They will calculate the risk and decide it is worth the try. Reward the risk takers because they are the ones who keep an organization moving along.

I am not talking about risk in the sense of a blind leap. But growth is, of necessity, going to involve making changes which involve some degree of risk. Human nature is to maintain the status quo. We are comfortable when all factors are known and there is no change. We can proceed down the same path we have been on for years, but that contributes to stagnation, not growth. To be innovative, to be creative, you are going to have to be willing to take a risk.

The willingness to take a risk—not a foolish one, but a prayerfully considered, calculated risk—is behavior which should be rewarded.

DECISIVE ACTION

James 1:6–7 says that the wavering man will receive nothing from the Lord—paralysis by analysis, you could say. People do not move because they are so busy analyzing the do's and don't's, the in's and out's. There is only so much analysis you can do. If you allow that analysis to be unbounded by reasonable limits, you will never make a decision. Frankly, it is better to make a wrong decision than no decision at all. You can correct a wrong decision. But making no decision causes you to stagnate.

Be decisive. That is a behavior worth reward.

SMART WORK, NOT BUSY WORK

The number of hours someone works is one of the things we tend to reward wrongly. Because someone works fifty or sixty hours a week, we reward them with compensatory time or time and a half, sometimes even double time. If that is the reward system you use, the people who have a tendency to work longer but not smarter will work fifty or sixty hours a week. On the other hand, if they do not get rewarded for their overtime, they find a creative way to squeeze the work down to forty hours. Believe me, it happens. Reward for smart work, rather than busy work.

SIMPLIFICATION, NOT COMPLICATION

Sometimes we think the more complicated our plan, the better our plan is. That's not true. You communicate better and respond better to something which is simple to understand. Most of what we do in management or in ministry can be simplified. Applied creativity will often address complicated issues. Creative thought produces a simpler way to accomplish the same tasks and improves efficiency.

The mail room may have done a certain thing a certain way; it was a good way when the mail room was handling so many pieces of mail or had so many employees. But things change, and if we are not careful, our tendency to maintain the status quo will not allow us to update our ways of doing things as we grow. We will wind up with a comparatively inefficient system.

QUIET, EFFECTIVE BEHAVIOR

Effective behavior is the key, but quiet, unassuming, unpretentious, effective behavior is worth a reward.

You have probably heard of the anatomy of an organization. There are the wishbones, the people who sit around wishing so and so wasn't their boss, or wishing things were different from the way they are.

Then there are the jawbones, the people who tell a good story and "spin a good yarn." They are the folks you avoid during the course of your day because they talk your ear off and waste your time.

There are the knucklebones, the people who knock everything. They rap everything that happens. They knock it down with criticism.

And then there are the backbones, the people you can always lean on because they support the ministry effort with quiet, effective and unassuming behavior.

CONSISTENCY

In every organization there are people you know you can give a job to, and consistently, week after week, they will produce. They always do what they say they will do—no hassles, no ands, ifs or buts. They consistently produce, and that is worth a major reward.

WORKING AS A TEAM

A lot of people have an interest in independently demonstrating how skilled and efficient they are. That isn't worth a reward nearly as much as those who show they can contribute to the overall effort and produce a corporate result. Value the team player over the independent producer.

POINT OTHERS TO JESUS

Remember, you are a more visible individual when you are the boss. When you are the leader of a department, people are going to look at you. Hopefully, you are orienting them toward Jesus.

Every now and then remind them that people have the capacity to let them down and disappoint them. Tell them to keep their eyes on Jesus. Remind them not to look too closely at you or they will see the spots and blemishes. Remind them of that particularly if they have a tendency to put you on a pedestal. Be aware you can either motivate the people who work for you or rob them of their desire to perform for you.

Personal Appearance

Because you are visible as a leader, here are some very basic considerations. You should inspire the kind of response you want from those working for you; therefore, personal appearance is important. I am so tired of hearing people say, "You need to see past the person to see the heart." Well, certainly, I am not interested in judging anyone. I am talking about your impact as a leader.

If it is obvious from your appearance that you are not a very disciplined person, your people are not going to be highly motivated to be self-disciplined either. They should see that your body is under control, that you care enough about how you look to dress well and groom properly. These things say volumes about who you really are and whether you are the kind of person they want to follow.

Personal appearance has more than a modest impact on motivating people you are leading to follow your direction.

Staying Fresh

During your private devotional life, spend time each morning praying about what He has called you to do. Let Him stir within you a fresh excitement about your participation in the plan of God. Share your excitement with those who work for you.

Reaping What You Sow

Then, of course, make sure you exhibit the character qualities we all want to see in those we serve:

- Integrity. Your employees must know you are honest and incorruptible.
- Loyalty. Your employees must know you are faithful to them.
- Availability. Your employees must know you are a resource to them.

- Sincerity. They need to know you are not going to backbite or belittle them when they are not around.

Corporations have spent millions of dollars to determine successful motivational forces they can employ to get better productivity from people. But the Bible tells us the most powerful motivating influence available to any of us. It is something that has been overlooked, for the most part, by secular managers. You will understand why. It is the love of God.

THE NO-FAIL STRATEGY

The Bible says love never fails. (1 Cor. 13:8.) Leadership is a relational skill. The Bible tells us that, in relationships, love never fails.

Why do we serve Jesus freely and with a glad heart? We are able to submit our lives to Him because we are confident of His love for us.

What makes submission happen in a marriage? The Bible tells husbands to love their wives as Christ loves the church. (Eph. 5:25.) The wife can submit to her husband because she is confident he loves her and will not abuse the authority which has been vested in him.

What do you think is going to make your people loyal, hard-working employees? It is the confidence that, because you are interested in them, you are not going to abuse your authority. You care about them.

NOT SOFT, BUT SINCERE

This does not mean you need to be soft on the principles which govern good business practice. It does not mean you should turn a deaf ear or a blind eye toward undesirable behavior. That is a misunderstanding of the love of God.

Love sometimes is extremely confrontational in the right way. Love produces a positive result in the person who needs to hear what you have to say. So it has nothing to do with being soft. It has everything to do with sincerity, having your people understand the motive of your heart, which serves their best interest.

When people become confident of your concern, your care and your love for them, you will be able to ask them to fly to the moon for you and they will.

We have talked a lot about rewarding right behavior. But the greatest reward we can offer and the most powerful influence we can exert on those we are responsible for is the love of God.

EPILOGUE

Leading a group of people is like dancing with a girl who is taller than you, smarter than you and who wants to lead. The problem is, you are the only one who hears the music.

Any success you achieve on the dance floor is necessarily going to be based on mutual cooperation; therefore, you essentially have three jobs to do.

First, you must convince her that you do indeed hear the music.

Second, you must demonstrate to her your ability to lead confidently.

Third, you must persuade her to follow your leadership instead of her own for the sake of the greater results cooperation will bring.

Likewise, as a leader in the Body of Christ, you must achieve the same three results with your people, whether they are a church congregation, a ministry organization or simply the folks in your circle of influence.

First, you must convince them you hold a vision for where they, as individuals or as a group, can go and also of a plan to get there.

Second, you must demonstrate a disciplined competency in leadership which confidently moves them toward the objectives.

Third, you must persuade them to follow your leadership, subjecting their vision to the larger vision you present, and making that vision their own.

If you can do this, God can use you to do anything within your vision—anything!

ENDNOTES

Chapter 5

[1]Vine, s.v. "honour," Vol. 2 pp. 230, 231.

Chapter 8

[1]Maxwell, pp. 171, 172.

Chapter 10

[1]Strong, "Hebrew," entry #3259, p. 47.

[2]Vine, s.v. "accursed" or "curse," Vol. 1, p. 262.

Chapter 11

[1]Vine, s.v. "life," Vol. 2, pp. 336-338.

Chapter 12

[1]Strong, "Hebrew," entry #7385, p. 108.

[2]Strong, "Hebrew," entry #1897, p. 32.

Chapter 18

[1]*American Heritage Dictionary*, s.v. "press."

Chapter 20

[1]Jacques, pp. 127-134.

[2]Strong, "Hebrew," entry #6612, p. 97.

Chapter 21

[1]Strong, "Greek," entry #4550, p. 64.

[2]Strong, "Greek," entry #3619, p. 51.

Chapter 23

[1]*Kronet,* pp. 53-57.

Chapter 25

[1]*American Heritage Dictionary*, s.v. "confront."

Chapter 28

[1]*American Heritage Dictionary*, s.v. "agreement."
[2]*American Heritage Dictionary*, s.v. "compromise."
[3]*American Heritage Dictionary*, s.v. "tradeoff."

Chapter 29

[1]Strong, "Greek," entry #191, p. 9.

Chapter 30

[1]Strong, "Greek," entry #53, p. 7.

Chapter 31

[1]*American Heritage Dictionary*, s.v. "communication."
[2]Vine, s.v. "logos," Vol. 4, p. 59.

Chapter 32

[1]*Lincoln.*
[2]*American Heritage Dictionary*, s.v. "manipulation."

REFERENCES

American Heritage Dictionary. Boston: Houghton Mifflin Company, 1982.

Jacques, Elliott. "In Praise of Hierarchy." Harvard Business Review. Boston: Harvard Business School Publishing, January/February, 1990.

Kornet, Allison. "The Truth About Lying." *Psychology Today*. New York: Sussex Publishing, Inc., May/June 1997.

Lincoln, Abraham. http://www.quoteland.com/html. 1997-2000.

Maxwell, John C. *The 21 Irrefutable Laws of Leadership*. Nashville: Thomas Nelson, 1998.

Strong, James. *Strong's Exhaustive Concordance* of the Bible. "Hebrew and Chaldee Dictionary," "Greek Dictionary of the New Testament." Nashville: Abingdon, 1890.

Vine, W.E. *Expository Dictionary of New Testament Words*. Old Tappan: Fleming H. Revell, 1940.

ABOUT THE AUTHOR

Mac Hammond is founder and senior pastor of Living Word Christian Center, a large and growing church in Minneapolis, Minnesota. Pastor Hammond also hosts a weekly one-hour television broadcast called *The Winner's Way, With Mac Hammond*, which is seen nationwide, and a daily sixty-second television commentary called *The Winner's Minute*.

Hammond has authored several internationally distributed books and is broadly acclaimed for his ability to apply the Word of God to practical situations and the challenges of daily living.

To contact Mac Hammond,

write:

Mac Hammond

P.O. Box 29469

Minneapolis, MN 55429

*Please include your prayer requests
and comments when you write.*

Other books by Mac Hammond

Angels at Your Service

Seeing and Knowing

The Last Millennium

Doorways to Deception

Available from your local bookstore.

HARRISON HOUSE

Tulsa, Oklahoma 74153

Additional copies of this book
are available from your local bookstore.

HARRISON HOUSE
Tulsa, Oklahoma 74153

THE HARRISON HOUSE VISION

Proclaiming the truth and the power

Of the Gospel of Jesus Christ

With excellence;

Challenging Christians to

Live victoriously,

Grow spiritually,

Know God intimately